P9-AZU-337

ABOUT THE AUTHOR

William Welch, late professor of political science at the University of Colorado, was educated at Harvard, Yale, and Columbia. He served with distinction in the Political Science Department of the University of Colorado for seventeen years and was associate director of the Honors Program for five years. Professor Welch also taught at Hamilton College in Clinton, New York; served as a research analyst for the federal government; had a fellowship at the Washington Center for Foreign Policy Research; and was a visiting professor at the University of California at Berkeley. During the academic year 1967-8 while on a faculty fellowship he traveled in Russia and other nations in eastern Europe. In addition to many contributions to scholarly journals, he was the author of *AMERICAN IMAGES OF SOVIET FOREIGN POLICY* published in 1970 by Yale University Press.

The following presentation was made in his honor on May 25, 1978:

"In grateful recognition of his unstinting faith in liberty of thought, freedom of inquiry, and the efficacy of education; for his abiding love and respect for his students; for the surpassing excellence of his teaching; for the exceptional quality of his published works; and for the humanistic model he cast for all of us: the Thomas Jefferson Award, established at the University of Colorado by the Robert Earll McConnell Foundation, is presented in the memory of William Welch."

THE ART OF POLITICAL THINKING

Government and Common Sense

WILLIAM WELCH

Edited by
Katharine S. Welch

Foreword by
Kenneth Boulding

1981

LITTLEFIELD, ADAMS & COMPANY

Library of Congress Cataloging in Publication Data

Welch, William, 1917-1978
    The art of political thinking.

    (Littlefield, Adams quality paperback; 362)
    Includes bibliographical references and index.
    1. Political science—United States—History.
2. Political participation—United States.
3. Abortion—Law and legislation—United States.
4. Discrimination in employment—United States.
4. Vietnamese Conflict, 1961-1975—United States.
I. Welch, Katharine. II Title.
JA84.U5W43   320   81-2834
ISBN 0-8226-0362-4   AACR2

Contents

PART II: GOVERNMENT IN THE SMALL

Foreword

In recollecting my many conversations with William Welch over the years, two characteristics stand out in my mind. The first is that one never went away from a conversation with him without in some sense being cheered up. The second is that one was always stimulated and went away thinking of new things.

This book, written with great charm and clarity, has the same two qualities. At a time of doubt and crisis, it is curiously cheering. It breathes a spirit of gentle and reasonable common sense which is very similar to the Jeffersonian ideals which the author espouses. It conveys a lively faith that with all of our falls from grace, the human race is capable of sensible political judgment and action, that we are not wholly at the mercy of blind anger and prejudice. The political culture, with all its abuses of power and mistakes of judgment, can call forth corrective activity.

The optimism of this volume is by no means untempered; there is a strong sense of how easily and how catastrophically things can go wrong. For this reason, the book is stimulating, not soporific. The examples of political controversy that the author uses to illustrate the principles of political thinking stimulate us to apply the same principles in our own thinking. It is hard to read this book without reexamining one's own position on these and many other issues about which one has given insufficient thought.

Conversations with William Welch are no longer possible, to our great loss, but at least in this volume he can talk to us. One longs to be able to talk back: "Look, Bill, you didn't put in enough about duties. You don't talk enough about the function of government in defining property. Economics is not just material things, you know; we do need to expand the concept of public goods. The concept of security has to be tied up with that of the dynamics of the threat system. How do you distinguish principles from policies?'' It would have been a wonderful conversation. He would come back, so gently, so reasonably, admitting some points and detecting one's nonsense. Now we can only hold this conversation within ourselves.

We owe Katharine Welch a debt of gratitude for bringing this manuscript into publishable form, for it is indeed one of the most attractive pieces of writing in political science that I have seen in a long time. It should be read widely, especially by young Americans, who can capture from it a real under-standing of what they have inherited and a capacity to build on that inheritance. One hopes also it will be read around the world by those who are curious about the contribution of this peculiar and remarkable experiment in political form and culture which the United States represents.

Kenneth E. Boulding

Preface

My husband had long felt the need for a book on political theory for the citizen. Like the founding fathers, he recognized the importance of the citizens' role in our democratic system and the need for them to improve their way of thinking about political issues. He believed that government would be more successful if citizens better understood the principles of political theory and applied those principles to contemporary matters.

This book is basically concerned with giving the reader two things: (1) an understanding of our great American political heritage—of the values on which our republic was founded and of the role assigned to government in preserving those values—and (2) a method for using this knowledge as a basis for reflecting intelligently on controversial political problems. In doing this, it provides insight into the thinking of the founding fathers when they established the republic and their reasoning for the restraints they put on government.

An exceptionally gifted teacher, my husband was noted in the classroom for his ability to distill the essence of thought from the myriad of details that frequently bog down persons of academia. He separated out the essential thought of the leading Western political philosophers and applied these principles to current issues. In this book he uses these skills to enhance the readers' understanding of our American system of government. It was his hope that this book would give both citizens and students of political science a better understanding of the role of government and help them cultivate the habit of intelligent reflection. Few readers, I suspect, will look at political controversy in the same way they did before.

Due to his untimely death from cancer in February, 1978, my husband was not able to complete this book himself. Too much work remained to turn the manuscript over to a fellow political scientist to finish and still keep it my husband's book. So it fell to my lot to try to take all the thought and beauty of the manuscript and put it in a form that would make it accessible to the reflective reader.

It was a most difficult undertaking for me but one I was determined to do since I believed deeply in my husband and in the importance of the work he was doing. I knew he had intended to condense the rather lengthy manuscript, to tighten the structure, sharpen the points, and fill in the gaps. In attempting to do this for him I have tried to keep as much as possible the elegance of his writing while making the changes needed to pull the material together. It is by necessity not exactly as my husband would have made it, but the thoughts and the spirit are all his.

During the eighteen months that I worked on the manuscript, I turned to many people for help—sometimes seeking detailed knowledge about a specific topic, other times seeking guidance on the overall manuscript, and finally seeking help in polishing the language. I cannot possibly acknowledge all the people who helped me in one way or another, but I am deeply grateful for every bit of help I got—both for the information and for the generosity with which it was given.

I am especially indebted to Professor Kenneth Boulding of the University of Colorado Economics Department for his reading of the manuscript, his suggestions, and his enthusiastic support. I am also deeply indebted to Alexander B. Adams of Rowayton, Connecticut, for his help, especially with the first chapter; he generously gave both his time and talent, in spite of poor health and limited energy. Others who were of great assistance include William Hitchcock, retired foreign service officer, whose careful reading and critique of the overall manuscript was most helpful in pointing the way to further changes needed, and Marianne Wesson of the University of Colorado Law School, who assisted with the legal aspect of the equal opportunity movement and the abortion question.

Special thanks go to Mary L. Hey for her valuable

assistance in editing the manuscript and for reading each paragraph for clarity and meaning. I also want to thank Eloise Pearson and her daughter, Chris Stilson, who took scratched-up drafts of individual chapters and overnight turned them into neat and accurate text. And lastly I want to thank my copy editor, Gladys Walterhouse, for her assistance in the final determination of material to be included.

My husband would want to acknowledge his gratitude to the University of Colorado for giving him a sabbatical in the year 1976-77. This leave from teaching duties made it possible for him to think out the format of this book, do the basic research, and write the first draft. He would also want to pay tribute to his early teachers and mentors who influenced him throughout his professional life: Payson Wild at Harvard, Cecil Driver and Whitney Griswold at Yale, Robert M. MacIver at Columbia, and Arnold Wolfers at the Washington Center of Foreign Policy Research.

And finally, since it describes so well the way this book was written, it seems appropriate to repeat here an earlier tribute given by my husband to my father, Elliott Dunlap Smith, one-time chairman of the Department of Economics at Yale. In the preface of my husband's book, *American Images of Soviet Foreign Policy,* he wrote,

> I gladly acknowledge a considerable debt to my father-in-law . . . who constantly urged the importance of starting the business of exposition and explanation not from the point which was most convenient to the expositor or which seemed right from the point of view of pure logic, but from the point at which the reader would seem most likely to catch on, and who constantly urged the virtues of brevity and reconcilement to a product short of impossible perfection.

My part in bringing this book to completion is dedicated to my husband—out of deep love and gratitude for all the blessings he gave me in the many years we shared together.

Katharine S. Welch

Introduction

Chapter I

Political Thought for the Citizen

"No government can continue good but under
the control of the people."

—Thomas Jefferson[1]

In November, 1979, the action in Tehran of unknown Iranian
students led indirectly to a fundamental constitutional question in Washington, D.C. a few weeks later. Scaling the walls
of the American Embassy, the students invaded the buildings and seized as hostages some fifty of the embassy
personnel. Normally the United States could have expected
the Iranian government to protect both the lives and the
property of its embassy staff, but times were not normal.
Relations between the two countries had deteriorated with
the exiled Shah's visit to New York, and the Iranian government was in a state of turmoil. It disavowed responsibility
for the students' action.

During the frustrating diplomatic impasse that immediately followed, American and Iranian students in
Washington, D.C. decided to stage a march to protest the
holding of the hostages. The Carter administration, believing
that a demonstration might result in injury to Iranian nation-
als in Washington and that this, in turn, might incite the
captors to kill some of the American hostages in Tehran,

---

1. Letter to John Adams, Monticello, December 10, 1819.

sought a restraining order. But the would-be demonstrators objected, claiming such an order would be a substantial infringement of their First Amendment rights.

On the one hand, the government wants to take a step it thinks necessary to protect the hostages' right to life. On the other, a group of citizens wants to exercise its right to freedom of speech and freedom of assembly. Both have rights under our constitution, but these rights clash. How can we rationally resolve such conflict?

*   *   *

A month later, far from the Moslem world of Iran, the city of Denver erected its traditional Christmas nativity scene on the steps of City Hall. A group of citizens protested, arguing that the use of public property for a religious display constituted a public endorsement of one particular religion and arguing that such endorsement violated both their own religious liberties and the First Amendment clause prohibiting the establishment of a religion. Those wanting the nativity scene replied that this was not the case, holding that it was a symbol of peace and universal love and, more importantly, that the purpose of the First Amendment was as much to prevent government from prohibiting a particular religious observance as it was to keep government from imposing one.

Two groups of people reach different interpretations of the same constitutional amendment. Which interpretation is more rational?

*   *   *

Some years earlier, the U.S. Bureau of Reclamation proposed the construction of a major new water development project on the tributaries of the Green River in Utah. This proposal, known as the Central Utah Project, called for the construction of several new dams, reservoirs, power plants, and pumping stations for diverting water across the Wasatch Mountains to Salt Lake City. This project, supported by industrial developers, farmers, and consumers who wanted additional water and electricity, was vigorously opposed by the ranchers who owned the land to be inundated and who recognized that they would be forced to move. They were joined in their opposition by local fishermen and hunters who wished to maintain adequate stream flow for trout and to protect the moose and elk. In addition several national conservation organizations opposed the project, fearing it would destroy the area's rock formations, its canyons, and its unique plant and animal species.

Once again two groups of citizens are in conflict, one claiming a right to water and power, the other a right to private property and environmental preservation. Which right should prevail?

* * *

In 1947, when the Communists threatened to take over Greece and Turkey, Harry Truman called Congress into emergency session and asked for authority to extend aid to these countries. "It must be the policy of the United States," he said, "to support free peoples who are resisting attempted subjugation by armed minorities or outside pressure."

His words signalled danger to many critics, Walter Lippmann and Hans Morganthau among them. Turkey and Greece were seriously threatened, they agreed, and this was a matter of concern to the United States. But they differed with Truman on the nature of the threat and the appropriate American response. The source of danger was not international Communism, they argued, but Russian imperialism. The problem therefore was local, not global, and the impact on the United States was indirect, not direct. The American response should thus be commensurably limited. The doctrine proposed by Truman, they believed, might lead to indiscriminate intervention around the world. The overriding concern of any foreign policy must be national interest, and the Truman proposal might eventually obscure this important fact.

Two groups of citizens—both of them responsible and

informed—disagree on the role of government in foreign affairs. How can we, as ordinary citizens, weigh the merits of these two positions?

*   *   *

These issues, arising in such wide-flung places as the Middle East and the middle United States, are examples of the many diverse controversial political questions faced by American citizens, whether they hold public office or are concerned private individuals. New issues arise almost daily. Some affect a relatively small number of people; others are much broader, affecting the whole country and having long-run national and international implications. Some involve relatively simple concepts; others, more complex ones. Some are purely political; others are primarily social or economic, but are political to the extent that they entail government action. All of them, however, involve conflicts of the basic values of life, liberty, and property. And they all center around this general question: when, how, and to what extent should government intervene to protect these basic values?

In a democratic system such as ours the answer to that question cannot be left to government alone; each citizen is responsible—at least to some degree—for helping to find it. For it is the participation of the citizens that distinguishes a democracy from other forms of government.

How does our democratic society handle controversial political issues? Frequently a public discussion develops, perhaps at a local town meeting or in a nationally broadcast debate between presidential candidates. Or the issue may be argued in letters-to-the-editor in a small-town newspaper, or at a hearing in the United States Congress. Usually there are elements of reasoning on both sides of the debate. Each side produces statements of support for its position, characteristically backed up by the citation of some facts and by some implied value judgments. And each side usually expands its original argument to include general facts and concepts that transcend the original problem. Too often, however, emotion clouds the debate. And too often the participants are blind to the full effect their proposal would have on their opponents or to the threat it poses to their opponents' values. This failure to recognize that what is good for one set of people may be bad for another impedes a rational analysis of the problem and blocks the way to a satisfactory resolution.

Is there not a better approach? Is there not a way we can develop a deeper understanding of the underlying concepts on both sides of an issue and their interrelationship? Is there not a way we can clarify, refine, and integrate these concepts and improve our process of rational thinking? The author thinks there is such a way, and this is to use a form of inquiry that is based on political theory.

Ever since Plato lectured to his students on government, great political philosophers have systematically described, analyzed, and criticized the activities of individuals and the role of government. And from this they have deduced some general concepts, based on a set of values, about politics.[2] These concepts, when organized into a coherent group, are referred to as political theory. They give us a basic understanding of political activity, of the relationship of government to the individual, and of the values we prize.

Usually political theories have developed from a desire to change, or to preserve, a given social and political situation. In the past when some existing political structure seemed wrong to political philosophers and they wished to find out precisely wherein it was wrong and hence how to right it, they inquired into the general principles of proper political

---

2. For those who desire a precise definition, I propose to define politics as a form of collective human activity directed at satisfying human wants of one sort or another. I propose further to consider political that social activity which is directed at manipulating persons in the service of general wants. I distinguish it from economic activity (which is directed at manipulating nonhuman phenomena in the service of material wants) and from cultural activity (which is directed at manipulating nonhuman phenomena in the service of intangible wants).

ordering. This would in turn take them back to the matter of origin. Such was the method used by many of the great Western political philosophers: Plato, Machiavelli, Hobbes, Locke, Rousseau, and Jefferson. Similarly, when an existing political structure that seemed right to political philosophers was being challenged and they wished to find out precisely wherein it was good, hence how best to defend it, they too inquired into general principles. Such was the case with Edmund Burke, facing the challenge to the English system represented by the French Revolution, and with Thomas Paine in defending, shortly after his arrival in America, the existing independence movement. So, too, was the case with the American theorists of international relations who worked out the black-and-white view of the world so widely accepted in the period of the Cold War.

The founding fathers relied on political theory when they were determining the reasons for declaring the colonies independent. They went back to certain general propositions about individuals before government existed, about the origin and purpose of government, and about its relation to individuals. From these they developed a series of more specific propositions on which they based their justification for separation from England. Jefferson organized these propositions in a pattern when he wrote the Declaration of Independence: "all men are created equal"; "they are endowed . . . with certain unalienable rights," including "life, liberty, and the pursuit of happiness"; "governments are instituted" by men "to secure these rights"; when "government becomes destructive of these ends it is the right of the people to alter or abolish it. . . ." Jefferson considered these such obvious truths and the pattern so logical that he called the Declaration the "common sense" of the matter.[3]

Like all good political theorists, Jefferson accented the general rather than the particular. For the theorist focuses on government as a whole or on certain classes of government

3. Letter to Henry Lee, May 8, 1852.

(such as democracy), dealing in abstractions instead of specific political facts (such as the American legislative process or the party system). The theorist refers to the particular only for the sake of exemplifying or testing hypotheses. And this is exactly what Jefferson did in the Declaration. Two hundred years later it still provides us with a fine model for the development of political thought.

By applying political theories to contemporary problems, we can arrive at a better understanding of the specific issues. This process, called "political thinking," requires going back to the basic values or principles on which a government has been established and building on them. It employs general law (or political theory) to arrive at propositions about specific cases. Its use is not limited to resolving current problems; it can also explain the past and help formulate future policies.

Political thinking is a thinking-through process, one that may be looked upon as a progressive process of clarifying concepts, ordering them, and reasoning upon them. It attempts to refine, integrate, and make explicit what previously was coarse, disorganized, and only implicit. The objective is understanding—the first step in a rational approach to problem solving.

Political theory is today as useful as ever in understanding contemporary social and political problems and reaching rational resolutions. Citizens—both those in public office and those who influence public policy through their writing, lobbying, protesting, or voting—need to return to the general concepts of government in order to reflect intelligently on specific problems.

The plan of this book is to lay out the pattern of concepts on which our democratic state was premised, specifically the general theories of John Locke and the founding fathers. In so doing the book examines only a small fraction of the total thought pattern that defines political theory, leaving out much that is important and worth examination. Yet it does identify the leading points of difference among theories of government—those having to do with the breadth of citizen participation, the scope of rule, and the means of rule. This undertaking brings us down to the meaning of basic concepts, to the roots of thought.

Together the theories examined provide a conceptual model of American democracy. Using this model as a guide the book proceeds to examine three controversial issues of the seventies. In each case the specific issue is analyzed, the important principles are identified, and these principles are tested against the theories on which our country was founded. The purpose is not to give a definitive answer to each issue studied, but to lay bare the canons of sound thinking. Finally the book sets forth a method for applying political theory to contemporary problems.

It should be emphasized that the three issues analyzed are presented only as examples for illustrating this process of inquiry. They are used to show the reader how he or she may go beyond initial sentiments and conclusions and identify the major factors on both sides of a controversy, and to show finally how the reader may systematically weigh and balance the values on both sides.

It should be recognized that there is no such thing as perfect truth and that there are no absolute answers to most specific issues. It is usually a case of the predominant evidence falling on one side or the other. It is also possible for two people to use the same rational thought process, yet reach opposite conclusions; they may start with different premises or make different value judgments. But even in a case where no agreement is reached, the process itself is valuable, as it forces inquiring persons to weigh the major values involved on both sides, and this leads to a better understanding of the nature of the problem. Intelligent reflection, although it cannot yield the perfect truth, will yield, if used by many people over a period of time, the best possible results.

It remains to be added that the author has tried to treat fairly the three controversial issues examined. No mind is utterly without bias and particularly so in such basic matters as one's outlook on political life. In the case of this book, the bias of the author is in the liberal direction. The author has tried to recognize this and correct for it, and he hopes he has succeeded. Similarly, he hopes readers will try not to let their own biases or their disappointment with some of the author's specific conclusions detract from understanding the basic approach to political thinking.

The purpose of this book is practical—to help readers find a method of clarifying their own thinking. It is not to give specific answers to specific issues but to show readers how to examine underlying concepts and to provide them with the tools for a rational approach to political controversy. The average person, it is fair to surmise, entertains implicitly at some lower level of consciousness the rudiments of a political theory. What normally he or she does not do is to clarify, refine, and integrate those concepts. This is the job that needs doing. It is to this end that this book is addressed.

PART I

Government in the Large

Chapter II

The Structure of Government: The Democratic Alternative

Government is a form of human organization. Understanding it, like understanding any organization, entails looking at it both in the large and in the small. Looking at it in the large means focusing on the more prominent features—the objectives that it claims as its goals and the more permanent characteristics of structure through which these ends are pursued. This is, as it were, the eagle's-eye view. Looking at government in the small means focusing on its particular year-to-year, month-to-month, day-to-day actions—particular elections, particular policies or laws, particular moves in the international arena. Here we have the mole's-eye view.

This book starts by looking at government in the large, with theories of what its ends should be, of how it should be organized to carry out those ends, and of what functions should be assigned or denied it. Specifically, the theory of democracy is emphasized, with prominent place given to its description and evaluation. The book then proceeds to look at government in the small, taking up three cases of particular governmental action. Each case involves a fundamental concept of democracy.

The plan of this chapter is first to define what we mean by government; second, to look at the basic characteristics of the structure and functioning of government in general; third, to define and differentiate what is meant by "limited democracy" in terms of these characteristics; and, finally, to expound on the principal form of "limited democracy" that has been handed down in our nation.

I. Conceptualizing Government

A. *The State Defined*

What is government? We must have an understanding of the fundamental elements before we discuss specific problems relating to the role of government.

Government, as I define it, is an association for protecting the very core of an individual's existence: life, limb, and freedom of movement. Threat to this core may come either from within or from outside the group, and the protection of this core may require force. Therefore government, as protector, normally acts in some measure coercively, through either the actual employment of force or the threat of it. In fact, protection through police and armed forces is frequently incorporated in its definition. Thus, the first purpose of government is to provide safety and security for the individual. This definition is for the minimal state.

But government serves other purposes as well, notably protecting private property and providing public goods and services. And in some instances it may serve still further purposes, such as controlling the economy. Some of these other purposes may be, and often are, incorporated into the general definition of government.[1] Yet, for clarity and simplicity, here we will stick with the sparer version noted: an association to protect the core of an individual's existence.

1. Some of these other purposes are often used to help distinguish types of government. For instance, a totalitarian government is by definition one that aims not only to provide safety and security, but also to operate and control the economic and cultural aspects of community life.

Diagram 1
STRUCTURE OF THE STATE

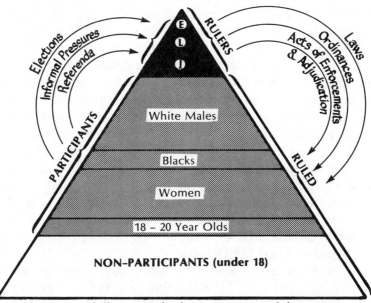

This pyramid illustrates the basic structure of the state, showing its division into the two groups of "rulers" and "ruled." Using the American democratic state as a model, the "rulers" are further divided into the executive, legislative, and judicial branches. The "ruled" are divided into those who participate in government (shown in the order they were given the vote) and those who do not participate (primarily those under 18 years of age). The "rulers" and the "ruled" are connected by lines of influence: on the left, the upsweeping arrows show how the participants are connected to the "rulers"; on the right, the downsweeping arrows show how the "rulers" are connected to the "ruled."

B. *The State Organized*

The association called the state is, like other associations, broken up into lesser groups with distinct roles. Of these the two most fundamental are the "rulers" and "the ruled." Each of these groups may then be further broken up as roles are further differentiated; leaders of government, for example, may be found in the legislative, executive, and judicial branches. The same individual may sometimes belong to one group, sometimes to the other. In fact, in the special sense that "no man is above the law," rulers are also among the ruled, Richard Nixon and Ronald Reagan being expected to abide by the rules.

Ruler and ruled, government and citizens, are connected in two ways: first, by lines of influence joining the latter to the former (elections, informal pressures, referenda, and the like) and, second, by lines of influence moving in the opposite direction (laws, ordinances, acts of enforcement and adjudication). See Diagram 1.

From the point of view of the individual citizen, there are three characteristics of the structure and functioning of the state that are particularly important. These are (1) the amount of citizen participation in the decisions of government, (2) the breadth or scope of government control over citizen activity (sometimes referred to as the "extensiveness of control"), and (3) the degree of coerciveness of the means of control (sometimes referred to as the "intensiveness of control"). See Table I. Clearly, it makes considerable difference to average citizens whether their government has little or a lot of citizen participation, controls a narrow or broad segment of their activities, or rules largely through persuasion or through coercion.

Let us be more specific. *Participation* may be open to all or a very large majority of the population (e.g., all adults). Or it may be confined to a small group encompassing only 1 percent of the subject population. Or it may be open to some segment of medium magnitude.

Table 1
CHARACTERISTICS OF THE STATE

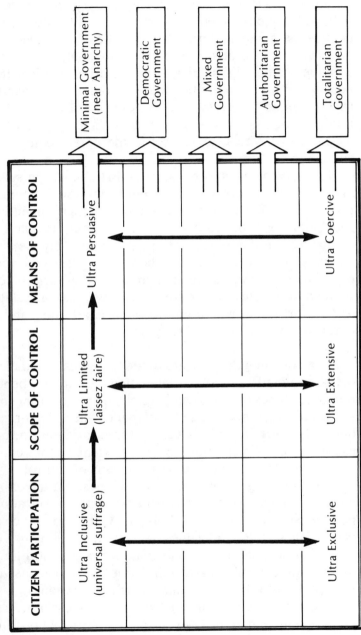

Scope of control, for its part, may be very limited, dealing only with the basic business of protecting life and limb that defines the minimal state. Or it may be broad, dealing not only with core protection of the individual, but with the activities of buying, selling, manufacturing, mining, transporting, and other activities that we commonly understand as "economic." Or it may be so extensive as to be virtually total, adding control over speech, press, and religion, indeed all citizen activities, to control of the purely political and economic.

Means of control may be minimal. In this case, persuasion and the milder forms of coercion (fines, etc.) dominate, procedural safeguards to the accused are prominent, and legislation is confined to what is general, regular, and equitable. At the other extreme, control may be deep, virtually unlimited. This is where the extreme forms of coercion like terror and torture abound, where legislation is secret and replete with ex post facto laws, class legislation, and so forth, and where enforcement is arbitrary and discriminatory.

Even confining the analysis to the three characteristics of the state noted, possible combinations are many; hence a number of types of states can be distinguished by using them. However, the problem can be simplified since, historically, one finds a correlation between the three variables: the more exclusive the participation, the more extensive the scope of control and the more intensive the means of control.

Using the degree of magnitude of these variables as a measuring stick, we can arrive at a working classification of political states, as shown in Table I. At the top of the scale we find a softness of values, a system ultra-inclusive in participation (marked by universal suffrage), ultra-limited in span of control (laissez-faire), and ultra-persuasive in means. I call this state minimal (nearly anarchic). At the bottom of the scale we find an extreme hardness of values, a government that is ultra-exclusive in participation, ultra-extensive in span of control, and ultra-coercive (terror-ridden) in means. I apply the term totalitarian to this state, Stalinist Russia being the example par excellence. Let us call the three intermediate types, in descending order, democratic, mixed, and authoritarian.

C. *Limited Democracy*

A democratic state is one in which many share in a rule that is moderate in both range and depth. A "limited democracy" is one in which that moderateness is enforced by clear-cut restrictions or boundaries. Put in practical terms, "democracy" as used in the phrase "limited democracy" means that most of the population is entitled to vote (and, let us add, to vote fairly frequently) and to do such things as run for and hold office, and serve on juries. "Limited" means that certain boundaries with respect to the substance of governmental action or procedure are recognized. These boundaries are typically accorded special status by incorporation in a fundamental document such as a constitution or bill of rights. Limits or boundaries are best known by the individual rights they protect. Limits on scope (substance) are marked especially by acknowledged rights of speech, press, assembly, religion. Limits on means (procedure) are marked by rights to a speedy trial and against unwarranted search and seizure, double jeopardy, and cruel and unusual punishment.

The hallmark of limited democracy, then, is a certain moderateness. The end is the modest, plebeian one of security, justice, welfare—something a bit more than that of security alone which marks the minimal state, yet something considerably less than that of molding the perfect society.[2] So it is also with the means, moderate in all three charac-

---

2. The implication here is that not only is total perfection unobtainable, but the search for it may lead to disaster, and that it is much better to seek a society characterized by reasonableness, limitations, and moderation. This is similar to the economist's notion of maximizing under constraint: to do as well as we can under certain limitations and to recognize that the limitations are really part of perfection.

teristics of the state. The many are to share, but not all; and those who share are to do so not directly but indirectly, by voting fellow citizens into or out of office. The scope of rule is to be modest, carefully restricted, and commensurate with the ends. And the means of control is also to be modest—coercion, lying behind rule as in any state, is to be exercised carefully within prescribed limits.

II. THEORY OF JOHN LOCKE

The theory of limited democracy as it has evolved in the United States is an extension of the theory of the celebrated eighteenth-century apologist for England's Glorious Revolution of 1688, John Locke. Locke's theory in its pure form, although it was neutral with respect to participation in rule, underlay the American Revolution. Amended by stages in the democratic direction, this theory inspired the organization of our political system in the 1780s and the changes accompanying subsequent crises, notably the Civil War and the Great Depression. And at each point of its evolution, the theory was embodied in a document or series of documents: the Declaration of Independence, which justified the Revolution to the world; the Constitution, which established the pattern of government; the Civil War amendments, which corrected the drift away from original principles; and the Supreme Court decisions that legitimatized the welfare programs of the New Deal.

John Locke's defense of limited government is set forth particularly in the second of *Two Treatises of Government*, dating from 1690. According to Locke, the only "true" state—that is to say, the only form of political organization that can justly claim an individual's obedience—is one that is highly restricted in function, scope of authority, and exercise of authority. Its *function* is confined to the securing of the rights to life, liberty, and property (which leads some commentators to speak of Locke's government as trustee in a trust relationship in which the people are both trustors and beneficiaries). The *scope of authority* is correspondingly confined and is not to extend, save in the most extraordinary circumstances, to the taking of property without consent. With respect to *exercise of authority*, the state is prohibited from acting except through clearly promulgated laws, applicable to all alike, and is prohibited from delegating this authority. To ensure these restrictions, authority is to be broken up into its critical legislative components and divided between independent agencies (understood then as Parliament and King).

Locke is neutral, as above stated, on the point of participation in rule, admitting the propriety alike of rule by one, rule by few, or rule by many. Actually, he inferentially accepts the modestly diffused pattern then characteristic of English government. This was one in which, along with the royal family (reflected institutionally in kingship) and titled aristocracy (reflected in the House of Lords), a role was assigned to the people in the House of Commons. "People", however, were confined to the untitled propertied freeholders, and excluded mechanics, artisans, workers, and, of course, women and children.[3]

Only in such a limited state, says Locke, is an individual obliged to obey. Toward absolute monarchy, such as Locke conceived the English state of the Stuarts to be, the individual has no obligation. And his obligation to the properly constituted or limited state lasts only so long as the limits, substantive and procedural, are observed. If the rulers exceed their mandate and enact legislation that goes beyond protection of individual rights or legislation that is arbitrary or inequitable, or if a man acquire office in violation of duly constituted procedures (thus becoming a usurper), or if rulers alter the duly constituted structure—then an individual is absolved from that duty. And a majority of such

3. Just as women were excluded from participation in government, so were they excluded from the language of Locke and the founding fathers. Therefore, in discussing their various writings and philosophies, I have retained the use of the words "man" and "men" for the sake of historical accuracy.

individuals have by right the authority to begin again and establish a new system.

Locke's justification for his theory is largely deductive. His scheme of limited power and limited obligation rests on the ground that government is founded on a contract stipulating such limitations. And his grounds for so arguing are that the only reasons for entering into such a contract are what he calls the "inconveniences" of the prepolitical order, the "state of nature." He sees this state of nature as one of natural equality among all men: that men, while free, are nevertheless restrained by the "law of nature." This law of natural morality teaches mankind that, being equal, one should not harm another. More specifically, Locke sees the state of nature as one in which men are born into the world as (1) individuals not subject to government, (2) individuals, moreover, possessed by nature of certain rights (specifically, life, liberty, and property), (3) individuals equal in possession of these rights, and (4) individuals rational and only moderately selfish.

And from this premise Locke argues that the only way one can then explain the origin of government is by supposing that men, being imperfect, differently interpret nature's law, apply it in a biased manner, and enforce it unevenly. This results in "inconveniences" marked by defects in the articulation, adjudication, and enforcement of a pre-existing law of nature. Men, recognizing this, see the setting up of a trust or contract with government as the logical way of improving enforcement of their natural rights. Conversely, given the premises, one cannot suppose that men would set up unlimited, absolute government, which would deprive them of rights available under the pre-existing law of nature.

III. THEORY OF THE FOUNDING FATHERS: THE DECLARATION OF INDEPENDENCE

The thought of the founding fathers on political matters was expressed in countless places—newspaper articles, public documents, public addresses, formal treatises, and private letters. The most representative of these are the Declaration of Independence and *The Federalist* papers. The founders themselves generally prized them as best summarizing their general political outlook.

The Declaration, though its words flowed almost exclusively from the pen of Thomas Jefferson, is the expression of the thought of a committee whose membership also included the illustrious John Adams and Benjamin Franklin; and it is also the voice of the Continental Congress. Its philosophic content is contained in its second paragraph, and especially in the following celebrated phrases:

> We hold these truths to be self-evident: That all men are created equal; that they are endowed by their Creator with certain unalienable Rights; that among these are Life, Liberty and the pursuit of Happiness. That, to secure these rights, Governments are instituted among Men, deriving their just powers from the consent of the governed; That, whenever any Form of Government becomes destructive of these ends, it is the Right of the People to alter or to abolish it, and to institute a new Government, laying its foundation on such principles, and organizing its powers in such form, as to them shall seem most likely to effect their Safety and Happiness.

Here now is familiar ground: the philosophy of John Locke. Governments are instituted—made, not born. They have as their sole objective the securing of pre-existing rights (although Jefferson substituted "the pursuit of happiness" in this document for the more familiar "property" espoused by Locke and most of the founding fathers). They can justly claim obedience only so long as they act toward these ends. Conversely, if they should act otherwise, in destruction of these ends, individuals are freed from their obligation and have the right to alter, abolish, start anew. Governments are so limited because this was the condition on which individuals gave their consent to form them in the first place. These were the terms on which they were

established, because originally men came into the world as
individuals, possessed of certain unalienable rights, rights
equally so possessed, and rights that cannot be bargained
away. And the only logical justification for the creation of
government is the securing of these rights.

The Declaration, like the theory of John Locke, does not
yet express the idea of limited democracy, as I have defined
it, in its fullness. Limits on government are not proclaimed in
so many words. The Declaration is neutral about form
(participation by the many in government is simply one
among others of the forms people may choose). Yet implicitly it exudes the idea of limitation. Limits on the state's
sphere of action are implied in that rights to life and liberty
can be given up to no man or political organization. Further
limits are implied by the right of the people to overthrow a
government that becomes "destructive of these ends." And
the acts of the King, delineated as the justification for our
separation from England, are clearly denounced as acts of
"absolute tyranny."

As for the "democratic" element, the Declaration, with
Locke, at least makes a step forward by treating "people"
(presumably operating by majority) as the source of legiti-
macy, and they are viewed as equal to one another in respect
to the relationship of rule. And though "people" continued to
be narrowly defined (confined no doubt to male freeholders,
thus excluding slaves and women, and possibly mechanics
and artisans), those meeting the definition in America constituted a larger percentage of the total population than was
the case in England.

The Declaration's philosophy is purely Lockean. Jefferson is reported to have rated Locke, along with Bacon and
Newton, as one of the three greatest men who ever lived.
And some of the phrases of the Declaration are lifted almost
verbatim from the *Second Treatise*. Locke's philosophy was
so widely accepted throughout the Western world in the
eighteenth century that the founders felt no need to argue it
at any length. It was simply, as indicated earlier, the
"common sense" of the matter.

The Declaration and its philosophy, apart from its content, are noteworthy for other reasons. In it, for example, we find the recognition of an important principle for the conduct of international relations: quite simply, what a future president of the republic-to-be would call "national self-determination." Though the Declaration appealed to a general right of revolution, it was not a call to restructure the British Empire; it was meant to be interpreted as the right of the American colonies to revolt—the separation of a part of the political order from the whole rather than reconstitution of that order.

The Declaration is also noteworthy for its form, one that matches well its substance. The document as a whole is, of course, something more than a philosophic tract. It is an announcement and justification of an important move on the world scene. It is a call for support—for support from within, among the uncommitted of the land, and from without, from sympathetic English people, from France, from Spain. For all this, its form, style, organization, and tone are of a high order. The document is tightly organized and the case beautifully molded. It is reducible ultimately to this syllogism: people have a right to revolt when their governments become destructive of their proper ends, which are securing the life, liberty, and the pursuit of happiness of said people; the King of England has become so destructive of these rights of the American people; the American people therefore have the right to revolt.

Finally, the Declaration is also remarkable for its tone. Although it is propaganda and contains its share of ringing phrases, it nevertheless has an air of reasonableness—a restraint that sets it apart, indeed far apart, from other revolutionary calls to arms.[4] Here is no vague and generalized diatribe against "oppression"; charges are particularized. With a single exception, where the British

---

4. One finds none of those indiscriminate, savage attacks on the "system" that pervade the Communist Manifesto, for instance, or the various declarations that accompanied the French and Russian Revolutions.

people are accused of being deaf to our pleas, these charges are confined to the British King rather than hurled indiscriminately against kingship or the British nation. And much of the sting is taken out of this exception by calling the British our "brethren" and by calling them, if "Enemies" in war, "Friends" in peace.

IV. THEORY OF THE FRAMERS: *The Federalist*

The Federalist is the second of the two great expositions of the political theory of the founding fathers. This is a series of eighty-five newspaper articles written between October, 1787, and May, 1788. In these, Hamilton, Madison, and, to a limited extent, Jay tried to persuade the people of the State of New York to ratify the United States Constitution, which had been recently drawn up in Philadelphia. They are thus primarily a campaign document defending the Constitution against its critics, but they are other things as well. They are, since Hamilton and Madison were two of the leading framers of the Constitution, generally considered the authoritative exposition of the political thought lying behind that document.

A. *Characteristics of Government under the Constitution*

The national system set up by the Constitution and defended in *The Federalist* has several major characteristics:
  (1) *Participation.* It is popular government, in that the people at large are declared to be the source of authority both for the structure of the system and for its operation. It is also indirect or representative popular government, people bringing their will to bear not by themselves directly enacting or enforcing law, but by electing representatives to enact legislation and electors to select an executive to enforce the laws.
  (2) *Scope of control (substantive authority).* It is restricted: the Congress enjoys enumerated powers

only, others being reserved to the states and the people, and is expressly forbidden to control certain activities (speech, religion, assembly, the press).

(3) *Means of control (procedural authority).* It is much restricted: the Congress may not suspend the privilege of the writ of habeas corpus, may not pass ex post facto laws, may not deprive persons of life, liberty or property without due process of law, and so forth.

As to the relationships of the leading agencies, the system is presidential in form. This form, according to the principle called "separation of powers," is marked by the allocation of leading types of authority (legislative, executive, judicial) to agencies largely independent of one another.

The Constitution also establishes the "federal" relation between national government and the states, this being a relation of rough equality—hence one in which the central government holds a stronger position than under the Articles of Confederation, but not yet a dominant one. And finally, the Constitution, while largely unconcerned with the interior structure and workings of the state governments, nevertheless stipulates they should be republican in form and restricted in certain ways, both substantively (no impairment of contract) and procedurally (no ex post facto laws, etc.).

B. *Limited Democracy: To What Extent?*

The government set up by the Constitution at first sight meets our definition of limited democracy. "Limited" it most certainly is, even if we leave the Bill of Rights out of consideration. "Democratic" I would also call it, in the main. For not only does the Constitution eschew rule by one (monarchy), but it forbids Congress to grant title of nobility and thereby prohibits the creation of a special class of citizens, which constitutes the traditional base for oligarchy. The Constitution further omits any special (i.e., property) qualification for holding office. And though the framers

certainly envisaged the continuance of property qualifications among electors, the Constitution is formally neutral on
this point. Representatives were to be chosen by the people
of the several states; the electors were simply to "have the
qualifications requisite for electors of the most numerous
branch of the state legislature." Persons meeting these
qualifications constituted a goodly portion of the population,
thereby answering to the term "many."[5]

But there are those who feel the Constitution is not
democratic; that the machinery of government set up by the
Constitution—the institutions through which the people are
to govern—is antidemocratic. These institutions are the
separation of powers, the checks and balances implicit
therein, the representative system, the federal principle, the
difficulty of the amending process, the comparatively long
term of senators, the indirect election of the President, the
presidential veto, life tenure for judges, and the practice of
judicial review. And these critics have a point. For part of the
purpose of these devices was to prevent the emergence of a
majority subversive to the order; or, if such a majority
should emerge, to impede its carrying out its will. The
framers saw popular government to be (like other forms of
government) something less than perfect, and the various
institutional devices pointed to were devised to counter its
characteristic imperfection.[6]

---

5. Senators were to be chosen by the legislature of each state.

6. Other objections have been raised against the claim that the Constitution is democratic. One school of historians, including the illustrious
Charles Beard, has insisted that it is an antidemocratic document,
marking a step backward from the Declaration. Part of the debate is purely
a matter of definitions. Some persons (and the founders were of this group)
confine the term "democratic" to one form only of popular government—the direct form in which the people themselves act as legislature,
as in the New England Town Meeting. The indirect form, which is
what the Constitution established, they call "republican." This is
perfectly defensible nomenclature. And so, too, is the above. But the
really important distinction lies between government that is popular
(government that in some way, whether directly or indirectly, is responsible to the people) and government that is not (that is responsible only to a
small segment thereof). And since we have come in our minds to associate
"democracy" with the good, and the good with the broader among these
alternatives, I have given it this definition.

C. *In Defense of the System*

1. *Rationale for Choosing Limited Democracy*

Why limited popular government? What was the rationale, in sum, behind the system established at Philadelphia and defended in *The Federalist*? But, first, why have government at all? The answer the framers gave now has a familiar ring. Government is set up "on the great principle of self-preservation, the transcendent law of nature and nature's God." Self-preservation—preserving one's life, liberty, and property against arbitrary incursions of another—is further depicted in *The Federalist* as society's "safety and happiness," and "safety" as avoidance of "foreign wars" and "domestic convulsion." Other objectives from time to time are recognized ("justice," rendered narrowly as the protection of economic interest and property rights). But one finds no mention of the classic ideas of "virtue" and "excellence." The accent remains on the rather negative idea of self-preservation, safety, and security, softened by the addition of the more positive "happiness." Or, put another way,

> To a very great extent, *The Federalist* determines the role of government with reference, primarily, to the extremes of external and internal danger. It is to avoid the precivil forms of these dangers that men form government, and it is the civil solution of these dangers which, almost exclusively, determines the legitimate objects of governments.[7]

But why limited popular government? The general problem in setting up the basic structure of government (the dilemma, if you will) is how to achieve government strong enough (Madison uses the term "energetic") to accomplish self-preservation without risking tyranny, such as the framers knew under the British. The answer *The Federalist* gives is several-fold. You make the new government strong by enlarging the powers enjoyed by the weak government of

---

7. Martin Diamond, "Democracy and *The Federalist*: A Reconsideration of the Framers' Intent," *American Political Science Review* (March, 1959).

the Confederation, by giving it independent authority and independent ways of acting on the citizenry, and by providing it with adequate taxing and other implementary powers. You meet the risk of tyranny (lawlessness in its most familiar and odious form) by opting for popular government. Then, in order to reduce the risk of lawlessness of popular government, you set strict limits to federal authority (in this case, in favor of both the state governments and individuals), arrange institutions so that terms of office shall be short, and arrange the several agencies of government so as to check one another.

Indeed, the special problem faced by the framers was how to achieve strong popular government without risking the much feared lawlessness. For the framers, one or two aside, were generally clear in their preference for the popular or republican[8] form; more precisely, they were clear in their rejection of the traditional alternatives of monarchy and aristocracy. Where monarchy was concerned, the reason was obvious: monarchy had given them George III. Where aristocracy or government by a few was concerned, the reasons were less obvious. Possibly the key reason was the one suggested by Jefferson: that the criteria customarily invoked for separating better from worse (birth, wealth) produced indifferent results (an "artificial aristocracy," he called it) that squared poorly with results achieved on more direct, intuitive grounds (the "natural" aristocracy).

The ordinary man, at least the ordinary man of some property, though incapable of understanding some subjects, was nevertheless not without some competence and character. And, moreover, he was capable of selecting out the more truly and naturally "better" among his fellows. Yet the ordinary man (like men everywhere of all kinds outside of a very few) also was prey to impulse and passion, and popular government might also turn into its lawless form— rule by mob bent on the likes of canceling debts and

---

8. A republican government is, in Madison's words, one "in which the scheme of representation takes place"; that is, one in which government is delegated to a small number of citizens elected by the rest.

redistributing property. And so *The Federalist* concludes that strong government must be not only limited in substance, limited in procedure, popular in citizen participation, but also modified in the operation of the popular element—i.e., indirect or representative government.

In its conceptualization of the origin and ends of government, *The Federalist* is Lockean along with the Declaration. But it goes beyond the Declaration in two significant ways. It goes beyond in particularizing the notion of limits. And it goes beyond by taking up a matter on which the Declaration is neutral, namely, the form of government, and opting clearly, if not fully, for the popular alternative.

2. Danger of Internal Factions

The danger, or as Madison puts it, the "dangerous vice," of popular governments is the propensity to violence of a "faction," and Madison deals with this in the celebrated tenth paper. "The instability, injustice, and confusion introduced into the public councils (by factions) have, in truth, been the mortal diseases under which popular governments have everywhere perished." A faction, Madison tells us, is "a number of citizens . . . who are united and actuated by some common impulse of passion, or of interest, adverse to the rights of other citizens, or to the permanent and aggregate interests of the community." And, says Madison, "the most common and durable source of factions has been the various and unequal distribution of property."

Factions may be dealt with either by removing their causes or controlling their effects. Removing causes is a matter either (1) of depriving citizens of their liberty, which nourishes the impulses referred to, or (2) of giving to all a single, uniform impulse. In the first instance, the cure is worse than the disease. And it is impracticable to give all a single impulse. As long as man's reason is fallible, there will be differences of opinion, attached to different impulses. And as long as men are of different and unequal faculties, they will come to acquire property in different degrees

and kinds. Rich and poor, creditor and debtor will perpetu-
ally contend with one another; these are opposing interests
that all but the most enlightened statesmen will be unable to
adjust and render subservient to the public good.

We are left, by the process of elimination, says Madison,
with the inference that the only way to cope with factions is
through controlling their effects. If the faction is a minority
one, there is no problem: the majority, or "republican"
principle, as Madison calls it, will deal with the situation.
With a majority faction, however, one does have a problem,
for the republican principle here forwards rather than frus-
trates its own objective. How can the majority be controlled?
Madison finds the answer in (1) the representative system
and (2) the scale of the polity. The representative system
"refines and enlarges the public views" by passing them
through the medium of a "chosen body of citizens" (a
proposition resting on the premise that representatives chosen by a given electorate tend to be better than average men).
And the size of the state also makes a difference: the larger
the system the better the chance of control. Extend the
sphere: the "greater the variety of parties and interests," the
less frequently "a majority of the whole will have a common
motive to invade the rights of other citizens"; or, if such a
common motive exists, "the more difficult for all who feel it
to discover their own strength and to act in unison with each
other."

The representative system, various other devices roughly
called checks and balances, and the large size of the new
nation (a fortuitous accident rather than a device of the
framers) are intended to keep that majority either from
uprising or from imposing its will tyrannically. And so to a
degree it is just to speak of Madison as antidemocratic. Yet
there are several severe qualifications that must be attached
to this judgment. First, the "mortal disease" of popular
government that Madison had in mind is an extreme one; he
gives the example of a majority actuated by a selfish interest
leading to "a rage for paper money, for an abolition of debts,

for an equal division of property . . . ." An effort to
equalize property can legitimately be stigmatized as subversive of the very political order, since the ends of government
assumed by the founders prominently included the protection of property. Second, the devices chosen are not in
themselves inconsistent with popular rule; they only make it
less direct, filter it, encourage better performance, and delay
implementation. Finally, the devices have another end in
view, the equally weighty objective of preventing the wrong
use of government. The fear of tyranny, despotism, and
oligarchy was even greater than fear of mob rule; the
prevention of degeneration into tyranny was an even more
prominent end then the control of the majority.

3. *Danger of War*

Where international affairs and American foreign conduct
are concerned, one finds a dearth of systematic theory. Yet
here again the framers were certainly not lacking in thought.
If Jefferson is typical, they conceived, as did Locke, of
international order as similar to the precivil order that
prevailed among individuals. International order was governed formally by a "law of nations," which Jefferson
coupled with the "law of nature" and understood as comprising peace, friendship, fidelity to treaties, and the like.
And in fact he found it governed by a system of customs
having peace as their objective. In reality, international
order, again like the precivil order prevailing among individuals, broke down from time to time and lapsed into war.
But, said Jefferson, the aggressor almost invariably met with
retribution. In a letter to Madison, he wrote: "No nation,
however powerful, any more than an individual, can be
unjust with impunity. Sooner or later public opinion, an
instrument merely moral in the beginning, will find occasion
physically to inflict its sentence on the unjust."

This concept is loosely analogous to the notion of "balance of power." And it is quite probable the founders
visualized the operation of a self-regulating mechanism such

as is conjectured by this venerable phrase. For not only had Hume's essay *Of the Balance of Power* appeared not many years before, but the idea had long held conspicuous place in political philosophy.[9]

The issue of foreign relations was of great importance in the minds of the framers of the Constitution. As already noted, the primary objective of government was self-preservation, and, of the great dangers to be preserved against—convulsion from within and war from without—the foreign was the more threatening. *The Federalist,* notably Papers Two through Five, deals with "Dangers from Foreign Force and Influence." They not only list the dangers, but they note the greater strength of the new union over the Confederation in guarding against these dangers. Danger #1 is the usual cause of just war (such as violations of treaties), and this the union would better protect against because of its greater efficiency and better character. Danger #2 is the usual cause of unjust war (such as invasion), and this the new union would better guard against by virtue of its greater ability to compel respect of other nations and prevent attack arising from jealousy over trade. Danger #3 is the alliance of an individual state in the union with a foreign nation, and this the new union would protect against by flat constitutional prohibition.

Besides the dangers of foreign war, there is the further danger of dissension among the states—civil war such as was to be realized seventy-five years later. *The Federalist* pointed out the destruction of life and property, the creation of standing armies, the extension of executive power, and the rise of military over civil authority that would result. The union would protect against this danger by building up its own armed forces and by providing machinery for the settlement of disputes.

---

9. The notion of checks and balances had been set forth by Machiavelli in *The Prince* back in 1513. And Locke had specifically espoused the theory of checks and balances. Furthermore, during the Enlightenment scientists, led by Newton, had conceived of the universe as operating after the fashion of a clock, the equilibrium notion occupying a central place in the mind of God.

Underlying all the above is the still further danger that military embroilment would undermine the internal order of limited republicanism, leading to a loss of liberty. *The Federalist* points to this constantly. In Paper #14, for instance, Madison hails the union as "our bulwark against foreign danger, as the conservator of peace among ourselves, as the guardian of our commerce and other common interests, as the only antidote to those military establishments which have subverted the liberties of the Old World." For the framers held ever in mind the close connection between foreign relations and internal stability.

D. *Method of Inquiry*

On the important subject of method (of what should be the proper focus and method of inquiry) the framers, while rarely delving into the subject with extensive system and care, held a view close to the prevailing view in eighteenth-century England—a view derived from Bacon, Locke, and Newton. In this view, the object of knowledge was generalization from imperfect particulars, not identification of the perfect truth or a nature-given answer. Bacon stressed the appeal to experience and saw truth as the outcome of a marriage between empirical and rational faculties—the result of a ceaseless reciprocal checking of idea against fact. As exemplified by the work of Newton and elaborated by Locke in his *Essay Concerning Human Understanding,* Baconism, or "experimental naturalism," aimed not merely at acquiring knowledge but at guiding action. This was an important part of the intellectual heritage of the framers.

Benjamin Franklin especially looked at things in the Baconian way. In inquiring into the physical realm, he joined the two types of activity Bacon had in mind—the elaboration of theory and the conducting of experimental tests—and doing so not only for the sake of understanding but also for the sake of taking action to improve the life of man. In moral questions he espoused a deliberate imaginative calculation of the expected advantages and disadvantages that would accrue from a particular option, with no pretense of quantifying the results. His recommendation was to tote up in adjoining columns all the pros and cons of a proposed course of action, wait a day or two, add hints about motive, then weigh pros and cons according to individual judgment, strike out balancing items as equally weighted, wait another day or two, and finally make the determination. Of the whole operation he writes:

> And, tho' the weight of Reasons cannot be taken with the Precision of Algebraic Quantities, yet, when each is considered, separately and comparatively, and the whole lies before me, I think I can judge better, and am less liable to make a Rash step. . . .[10]

Among the other framers, too, one finds expressions of what I loosely call Baconism. All or almost all of them express an interest in developing a "science of politics," and this implies agreement with the method outlined above. They understood the product of scientific endeavor to be something considerably less than the perfect truth that many have since ascribed to it. John Adams is conspicuous in his regard for this science of politics.

Madison, in the 37th paper of *The Federalist,* makes a number of interesting comments in this regard. He describes the outlines of a proper inquiry into the subject under consideration (which, of course, was the merits of the constitution he and his collaborators were recommending to the people of the state of New York) and inferentially the outlines of the endeavor to develop a science of politics. He first stresses the importance of making "a more critical and thorough survey of the work of the Convention, . . . examining it on all its sides, comparing it in all its parts, and calculating its probable effects." Criticizing, looking at both sides, comparing, calculating consequences: these are the first desiderata for proper inquiry.

Next, Madison says that a "spirit of moderation" is

10. Benjamin Franklin, letter to Joseph Priestly, September 19, 1772.

"essential to a just estimate of (the) real tendency (of public measures) to advance or obstruct the public good." Though this is hard to achieve and rare in human experience, it is nevertheless, he clearly implies, not impossible. Madison then connects with it the control of bias, the "predetermination" of one or another finding. An important subject such as the adoption of a constitution invariably excites "unfriendly dispositions" on one side or the other. Such predeterminations, certain of which Madison finds excusable and certain others inexcusable, are inevitable in some people. Yet in others this is not so, and it is to these other people— "those . . . who add to a sincere zeal for the happiness of their country, a temper favorable to a just estimate of the means of promoting it"—that the arguments of *The Federalist* are addressed. These people will not only allow for errors in the Constitution chargeable to the fallibility of its authors, but "will keep in mind, that they themselves also are but men, and ought not to assume an infallibility in rejudging the fallible opinions of others." Thus, a spirit of moderation or allowance for one's bias is the second desideratum for proper inquiry.

The next topic Madison brings up is the complexity of the subject matter; criticizing and evaluating competing governmental patterns is a difficult matter. One has to rely on past experience, seeking to avoid the errors this suggests. But the past does not speak unequivocally, and so one is bound, even with the best of effort, to commit new errors in attempting to rectify the old patterns of government, and the most one can do here is "to provide a convenient mode of rectifying" these new ones "as future experience may unfold them." The emphasis here is on consulting past experience, and recognizing its insufficiency to provide a perfect guide to the future; hence, the emphasis is also on the need for providing some mode of self-correction. Madison illustrates the complexity of the problem by showing how difficult it is to reconcile the demands for strength in government, on the one hand, and liberty on the other.

Madison then generalizes on the difficulty of drawing

boundaries. The first task in the development of knowledge is the business of definition. Yet how difficult it is! The problem is exemplified by the vagueness of the lines separating the provinces of the "science of government": legislative, executive, judicial. As Madison put it, "Questions daily occur in the course of practice, which prove the obscurity which reigns in these subjects." The problem is threefold. There is first the obscurity arising from the complexity of the object itself. Second, there is the obscurity arising from the imperfection of human faculties. Finally, there is the obscurity arising from the medium of communication, namely, the use of words. "Clear and distinct ideas, clearly and distinctly expressed"—these are the final desiderata for proper inquiry.

In Madison's view, the right use of the mind in pursuing inquiry connected with the science of politics, whether theoretical or practical, may be summarized as follows:

(1) Start with clear and distinct ideas, clearly and distinctly expressed.

(2) Frame alternative courses, attending critically to each.

(3) Compare with respect to calculated consequences, relying on past experience.

(4) Maintain a spirit of moderation, discounting one's biases.

(5) Remember that the final product is at best imperfect, and make provision for correction on the basis of future experience.

The founders to a remarkable extent practiced what they preached. If one takes almost any paper in *The Federalist,* or, for that matter, the set as a whole, one finds that they have followed the method of inquiry set out above. The alternatives are clearly set forth in the aggregate (government under the Constitution versus government under the Articles of Confederation) and definitions are clear (e.g., definition of "faction"). The two alternatives are constantly compared with respect to their projected consequences on values such as strength, stability, liberty, and external and internal peace. Experience—the record of past democracies, past confederations—is continuously invoked. Discussion is conducted in a moderate spirit, Madison and Hamilton rarely if ever raising their voices. And although in a sense one can say bias is evident (the document being after all a campaign document), bias rides none of the authors. For a campaign document, the papers are astonishingly lacking in the evocative, honorific, or pejorative language and in the polemics we normally expect to find in such documents. Finally, conclusions are presented with remarkably little dogmatism; rather they are offered as the best solutions in this complicated and imperfect world. And provision is made for their correction against future experience.

Let me conclude this subsection with a few thoughts taken from Arthur Schlesinger. The statesmen of the revolutionary period were Lockean to a man. Their dedication, as Locke's, was to the values of individual rights, liberty, popular sovereignty, and private property. But also like Locke, their bent of mind was empirical; that is, while incorporating these values into the new order they were constructing, they were ever cognizant of experience, of the historical record. Differences there were, and sharp ones, between Hamiltonian partisans of a strong government, one favorable to industry, and Jeffersonian supporters of a weaker government, one favorable to an agricultural economy; between leaders like Marshall who was partial to strong national government and those like Calhoun who favored decentralization. But these differences were debated within a consensus that took Locke for granted.

V. THEORY—POST 1791

Since the establishment of limited democracy at Philadelphia, the meaning of the Constitution has continuously evolved, through amendments, legislation, and Supreme

Court decisions. But there have been few if any changes in the formal structure of our government that could legitimately be described as drastic. Most of these changes have been in the form of amendments, and of these, three types in particular come to mind.

There are, first, the changes that amount to *the enlargement of the participants* in government and of the modes of participation. Groups initially disenfranchised under state and national constitutions have become enfranchised: the nonpropertied, the blacks, women, and youth aged 18 through 20, in that order. In most states, modes of participation have been increased by adding devices of "direct democracy," such as the initiative, referendum, and recall.

There is, second, *an expansion of the scope of government*—an increase in the number of activities it undertakes, whether negative or positive. While the founding fathers were never so sparing in advocating the exercise of power as once was thought (for example, Madison and Jefferson were the leaders in the movement for state education), their activities loom small compared with those of their descendants. One finds in those earliest days little support for the regulation of the economy known today, and virtually none of a welfare nature. In this case, augmentation has come about less by way of amendment, more by way of judicial legitimization. Also probably to be counted here is the prohibition of slavery memorialized in the Thirteenth Amendment, but some may question whether on balance this amounted to an increase or a diminution of governmental activity.

There is, third and finally, *an increase in the restrictions on the means of control,* particularly restrictions on procedural authority. Governments, both national and state, have come to be required to act more equally (prohibited from denying "equal protection of the law" and from discriminating in voting on grounds such as race or sex) in the face of pressure from diverse groups in the population. And governments have come to be more restricted in their handling of those accused of breaches of the law. Here the change has been brought about partly by amendment and partly by judicial enlargement of existing provisions.

These three sets of changes constitute a solidification of limited democracy. Two of the three amount to the strengthening of the two elements that distinguish this type of government, the "democratic" and the "limited": the "many" have become more numerous, a greater proportion of the whole, and more participatory; and limits to authority have become stricter. As to the scope of authority within these limits, a subject not spelled out clearly in the earlier days, the increase is not inconsistent with the concept of limited democracy.

Thought normally accompanies practice, sometimes leading, sometimes following. And changes in American political thought have likewise been far short of drastic. Indeed, limited democracy remains even today the dominant pattern in that thought, with the concept of "people" expanded. The ideas of Locke and the founding fathers ("meliorism, progress, liberty, equality, democracy, and individualism," united in the notion of government as servant of the people) even today habitually organize our thinking on political subjects. And on the major point of the superiority of popular government, the rejection of government by the few, the framers stand leading the way.

On the whole the reasoning underlying American political theory has remained the same. Many theorists have come to rest their case for democracy on the innate goodness of the average man, although most have discarded the contract interpretation of the origin of government. While in the main retaining the rationale of the founding fathers, theorists have at points supplemented and elaborated upon it.

This is not to deny the existence of important differences and conflicts between theorists. Most notable here is the difference between those, on the one hand, who stress limits favoring private property and a laissez-faire economy and who defend as inevitable or desirable the existence of wide inequalities in wealth, income, and so forth and those, on the other hand, who stress limits favoring freedom of speech, press, and assembly, and who defend efforts to curb inequalities. Also there is the conflict between those who argue for a strong, active, interventionist role in international affairs and those who argue for a restricted role. But these differences, as those between Hamilton and Jefferson, do not affect the fundamental postulates, on which agreement remains. Disagreement revolves around the relative weights to be given the various values rather than around the values themselves.

VI. CONCLUSION

Limited democracy is government of the many, restricted in scope and means. Widespread participation, though it may be exercised in a number of ways, today primarily takes the practical form of frequent election of rulers by universal adult suffrage. Substantive limits take the form of restrictions to protect basic freedoms. And procedural limits take the form of such restrictions on legislative power as prohibitions against ex post facto legislation, and such restrictions on the executive and judicial power as prohibitions against suspension of the writ of habeas corpus, deprivation of life and liberty without due process, and denial of jury trial. Defining features normally are embodied in a written constitution.

The theory of limited democracy argues its case in a number of ways. Proceeding deductively, it argues that legitimate government can rest only on consent, and given human nature as we find it in the absence of government (and the resulting social conditions), we must conclude that consent would only be given to a government of limited functions and authority. Appealing to experience, it argues for the democratic element on the grounds that (1) the presumption lies in its favor, and that (2) when participation is restricted, there is no assurance that rulers of sufficient virtue and wisdom to retain the consent of the masses will be found.

The theory of limited democracy is the American political theory par excellence. It is an extension and refinement of John Locke's theory of limited government. This adapted theory is largely the work of the founding fathers, who appealed to it as justification for the American Revolution and took it as a guide for the erection of the political order enshrined in the Constitution. Subsequent writers have altered the rationale but little. Americans at large have accepted it in its major assertions for almost two hundred years.

The American theory of limited democracy is a moderate theory—moderate in all ways. It provides for popular participation but not too much; it provides power to those who govern but not too much. It is premised on a moderate view of human nature—the human being as a moderately selfish, passionate animal, yet with a touch of character and capacity for enlightened self-interest; limited insofar as the reach of the mind is concerned, but endowed with some common sense. The end objective is that of making life a bit better, a bit more civilized rather than that of realizing a heaven on earth.

The purpose of setting forth and discussing the theory here is only partly to acquaint the reader with the dominant political thought pattern of our country. It is also to provide some sort of guide to the resolution of particular problems of the day. To illustrate how this can be done, I have chosen three controversial issues, each involving a fundamental value on which our government is premised: liberty, equality, and security. I propose to consider these issues in the following chapters not only from the point of view of what intelligent reflection suggests to be their solution, but also in light of the doctrine upon which our political system rests.

The founding fathers believed in the natural intelligence of the ordinary man and in his capacity to learn. They have given us the principles of democratic government. And they have shown us the fundamentals of intelligent reflection. Together these constitute the essential tools for "government and common sense."

PART II
Government in the Small

Chapter III

Government and Liberty: Abortion

Citizens who are concerned with their government and undertake to judge its activities soon find that to make such judgments they must consider the term "liberty." A leading reason why the people of the United States established the Constitution and the political institutions described therein was to "secure the blessings of liberty to ourselves and our posterity." Rather commonly, proposals for laws, laws themselves, enforcement procedures, and executive action (other than that of pure enforcement) are justified in the name of liberty. Quite as commonly, they are rejected in the same name.

I. The Case

The abortion controversy is a good vehicle for seeking an understanding of liberty and the relationship of government to citizen that liberty involves. On some cosmic view, the state's role vis-a-vis abortion may not be the most important issue confronting the republic. But the issue serves admirably our purposes here because it has been widely publicized, and is still timely, and because the debate on it illuminates with unusual clarity the difficulties that confront citizens seeking a satisfactory balance of authority and freedom.

The abortion issue has many facets, such as the different

circumstances of conception, the different conditions of the pregnant woman and the fetus, and the different stages of pregnancy. Central, however, is the question of whether or not the state should prohibit abortions. And in this particular case study, I have chosen to limit the question to whether or not the state should prohibit abortion *in the first trimester* of pregnancy for reasons less urgent than conception through rape, the prospect of deformity of the fetus, or risk to the health or life of the woman. In other words, should the state prohibit abortion in this period for a woman who simply does not want a child? Since the Supreme Court in January, 1973, ruled that under our Constitution state governments cannot prohibit abortion in the first trimester for any reason at all, the debate today often centers on the question of support for or opposition to this decision, and often too, support for or opposition to a proposed amendment to the Constitution which, in effect, would overturn this decision.

The plan for this chapter is to set before the reader a series of characteristic "statements of position" on the issue and to submit them to preliminary criticism. This criticism will suggest difficulties in the reasoning behind these statements and show the need to analyze the basic concepts involved in order to come closer to the resolution of the main issue. There follows an analysis of liberty, rights, and the status of the fetus and, subsequently, of the Court's interpretation of these. Returning to the resolution of the main issue, we then formulate exemplary patterns of intelligent reflection and finally raise the question of their adequacy.

II. GENERAL ARGUMENTS

A. *Statements of Position*

The lay person is likely to encounter the abortion issue in news reports on Court decisions, reactions to such decisions, public speeches, statements of interested organizations (such as the Right-to-Life Committee and the National

Abortion Rights Action League), and bills in state legislatures and public reactions to them. Necessarily, statements of positions are usually abridged, and what one reads therefore probably does not fully reflect what goes on in the minds of the authors. But what one reads may nevertheless be taken as reasonably representative of the range of viewpoints. We have now to consider the validity and the adequacy of a random sample.

Here, taken from a file of such reports amassed through the years by the author, is a series of characteristic statements.

Statement #1. "The [Supreme Court] ruling drastically diminishes the constitutional guarantee of the right to life, and in doing so sets in motion developments which are terrifying to contemplate."[1]

Statement #2. "[The decision is] a wise and courageous stroke for the right to privacy and for the protection of a woman's physical and emotional health. . . . As a nation we shall be a step forward towards assuring the birthright of every child to be welcomed by his parents. . . ."[2]

Statement #3. ". . . the majority of the Court bowed to outside pressure. . . . The long held belief in the absolute value of each human being, and his right to live, has been discarded. . . . The unwanted child is a misleading issue. Women's attitudes fluctuate during pregnancy; the unwanted pregnancy often ends up being a wanted baby. . . . Ninety percent of battered children were planned pregnancies."[3]

---

1. Cardinal Krol, president of the National Conference of Catholic Bishops, *New York Times,* 23 January, 1973, p. 36.

2. Dr. Alan F. Guttmacher, president of the Planned Parenthood Federation of America, *New York Times,* 23 January, 1973, pp. 1, 20.

3. Dartt Demaree, member Boulder Right-to-Life group, citing statistics from Dr. Edward Lenoski, University of Southern California, *Colorado Free Observer,* 26 January, 1973, p. 4.

Statement #4. "[The] decision dealt with a question apparently of little concern to anti-abortionists. . . . the rights of the mother. . . . The mother is not an inanimate tin can, or an egg, whose only importance is to perform a biological purpose. . . . The court deserves praise for its decision in upholding freedom of choice for a woman saddled with an unwanted pregnancy."[4]

Statement #5. "The vast majority of Protestants and Jews as well as many Catholics defend the constitutional right of free choice in abortion as defined by the Supreme Court."[5]

Statement #6. "He said he was saddened to see Boulder allow the establishment of an [abortion clinic] . . . responsible for the selective killing and slaughter of more than 1,000 pre-born babies. . . . The United States is founded on the inalienable right to life. . . . Yet selective destruction of life is now beginning with the youngest—the unborn. Who is next?"[6]

Statement #7. "A new report by the National Academy of Sciences affirms the wisdom of the Supreme Court's 1973 decision. . . . [It] clearly shows that legalized abortion has been a 'major factor' in reducing the frequency of infection and death commonly associated with the old back-alley abortion mills."[7]

Statement #8. "[A physician can do no higher good than to] help a pregnant woman weed out her unwanted and ill-formed embryo."[8]

4. E. Thomas McClanahan, editor of *Colorado Free Observer*, in *ibid.*, 23 January, 1973, p. 4.

5. Methodist Bishop John Wesley Lord, citing Gallup Poll finding that 64 percent of Americans considered abortion a private decision between a woman and a doctor, *Rocky Mountain News*, 2 February, 1974, p. 122.

6. Attributed to Richard Francis, past president of the Colorado Right to Life Committee, *Rocky Mountain News*, 4 November, 1974, p. 5.

7. Editorial, *Rocky Mountain News*, 2 June, 1975, p. 46.

8. Dr. John C. Cobb, professor of preventive medicine at the University of Colorado Medical School, *Rocky Mountain News*, 15 January, 1976, p. 32.

Statement #9. "[Those who deny a society's responsibility to protect each human life as precious] open up the gates—as Hitler did—to making the decision who shall live and who shall die. Buchenwald, Dachau, Auschwitz—they say that it could never happen here. But it has already happened. It is happening all around us right now. Since January 23, 1973, three million lives have been destroyed."[9]

Statement #10. "Making it [abortion] illegal makes it expensive and dangerous; it won't stop it, probably won't even slow it down."[10]

Statement #11. "Abortion is none of the government's damned business."[11]

The above statements are highly varied in content and tone. They are statements about abortion itself, about state prohibition, about the Court decision on the constitutionality of state prohibition; they are statements affirming or disclaiming "facts"; they are statements about a certain kind of legal "right"; and they are statements of value (affirming something to be good or bad) and statements of "logic" (drawing one alleged truth from another). They present a fair sample of the kind of data that first alert you and me, citizens, to the abortion problem and constitute the raw material of reflection.

B. *The Positions Criticized*

How do we deal with these data? How do we make sense out of these conflicting opinions and bring order to the blooming, buzzing confusion of words and thoughts about

9. Cardinal Cook, Roman Catholic archbishop of New York, *New York Times,* 23 January, 1976, p. 20.

10. Columnist Nicholas von Hoffman, *Washington Post,* 19 April, 1976, p. C1.

11. S. I. Hayakawa, former president of San Francisco State University and later a U.S. Senator, *Colorado Daily,* 27 October, 1976, p. 9.

abortion? Let us first examine each one of the statements, asking how much sense each makes and how convincing each is.

Statement #1 supports prohibition of abortion on grounds that the unborn has a constitutional guarantee of a right to life (in effect claiming the Court has misread the Constitution). It appeals to a "right" said to be embedded in an authoritative body of fundamental law. Must we assent? There are two problems. First, are we certain this right in fact exists? For, as a casual glance at the Constitution will show, references to a "right to life" occur only in a qualified context, deprivation thereof being forbidden "without due process of law." Second, is the position complete? If we grant there is a right to life, does it apply to the unborn—to the nonviable fetus? And is this the only right at issue? Finding no clear answers at hand, we must suspend giving assent.

Statement #2, by contrast, opposes prohibition (i.e., supports the Court and abortion) on the grounds of the right of privacy of the woman. This appeal is of the same kind as the preceding, except it here invokes an alleged right of the opposite party. Again, we may grant the existence, if qualified, of the right referred to. But must we assent to the position? Again, no, for the reflective citizen must ask, "But why must the woman's right outweigh the unborn's? And how do we balance the two?"

Statement #2 also, however, elicits our support for abortion on the quite different grounds of considerations of the woman's physical and emotional health. The implication here is that a woman bearing an unwanted baby faces either a distressful life and future or, should she decide to terminate her pregnancy, the medical risks and emotional horrors of a back-street or self-induced abortion. The appeal here is to probable future consequences, rather than rights. Must we assent? To the assertion that these things may follow—yes, probably. But to the conclusion as a whole, no—again on grounds of incompleteness.

Statement #3 bids for our support for prohibition (against the Court). The grounds are both those of right (normative) and of fact (empirical). Appeal is, on the one hand, to the "absolute value of each human being, and his right to live." On the other hand, appeal is to consequences. More specifically, the contention is that the effects of bearing the unwanted child are by no means as extensive as pro-abortionists affirm. Evidence is presented. Shall the mind assent? The answer is no. On the appeal to the right of the fetus, the statement ignores the rights on the other side. And, on the appeal to consequences, it ignores the question of how often pregnant women might change their minds. Finally, on one point the reasoning is defective: the fact that 90 percent of all battered children were wanted babies does not of itself mean, as implied, that the unwanted child does not stand a higher chance of being battered.

Statement #4 reaffirms the rights and freedom of choice of the prospective mother. Besides bearing the usual infirmity of insufficiency, it also uses misleading language. It is hardly fair to charge the opposition with regarding the mother as an "inanimate tin can"; and to speak of a woman's being "saddled" with an unwanted pregnancy implies that she had nothing to do with bringing on her condition, which is normally incorrect.

Statement #5 grounds its support for abortion on the alleged fact that the vast majority of members of all faiths support a woman's right to choose. The authority cited is a Gallup Poll. Must we concur? No. Granted the authoritativeness of the source and the reliability of this statistic, the reasoning is again defective. That a majority supports a measure may make it legitimate, but it cannot make it right in the sense we are exploring. The error exemplifies a kind of mistake in reasoning known to logicians as an *argumentum ad populum*.

Statement #6 asks us to oppose abortion. The grounds are that our political system recognizes the right to life; that abortion represents not merely the taking of life, but "slaughter"; and that this destruction is the first phase in a process bound to extend to other classes in the population. Here two new elements lead us to question thè reasonableness of the argument and to withhold assent. One is the characterization of abortion as "slaughter," for this is an appeal directly to the emotions and hence inimical to sober reflection. The other is the allegation that the destruction, once started, will be likely to spread, a claim for which there is no ready support. Nor can there be, for this is what Professor Sidney Hook calls a "slippery slope argument," one equally usable on both sides of an issue.

Statement #7 asks our support for keeping abortion free of state control on the grounds that since January, 1973, there has been a marked reduction in infections and death formerly associated with the back-alley mills. Here is a new consideration—the problem of the enforceability of a ban on abortion and the indirect effects of such a ban. Whether one accepts the evidence depends on whether one accepts the authoritativeness of the sponsoring institution. If one does accept the institution's credentials, one may venture a cautious yes.

Statement #8 invites our support for doctors helping in abortion, and inferentially for abortion itself, by unabashedly terming "good" the "weeding out of an unwanted and ill-formed embryo." Should we assent? I think not. Apart from incompleteness, the language used (specifically, the phrase "weeding out") is subject to an objection similar to that against "slaughter," namely, it is provocative. Trivializing abortion as of no more consequence than uprooting noxious plants from one's garden discourages sober reflection.

Statement #9 calls for prohibition on the grounds that failure to protect each human life will open the gates, as Hitler did, to state decisions on who shall live and who shall die. Must we agree? No, again. For reason here has quietly slipped her moorings. The analogy to German concentration camps is quite false—for what else can one say to likening the destruction of three million embryos, acts separately performed by private individuals, to the state-executed mass killings of Hitler's concentration camps? And the stark claim that legalized abortion opens the gates to removal of controls on the taking of human life is another example of "slippery slope" reasoning.

Statement #10 elicits our opposition to prohibition by turning attention again to the matter of enforceability. Whether good or bad, you can't stop it, argues the writer, and in trying to, you only force it to take place under conditions much more dangerous. Must we assent? Here we have a statement of judgment, and we must depend upon our assessment of the writer's reliability as a reasonably unbiased observer.

Statement #11 makes the point that, right or wrong, abortion is not within the purview of state authority. This provokes the response, "Why not?" For if abortion can be considered taking life (as it is from one point of view), should not the state, whose first job is to protect the life and safety of its members, be entitled to step in and stop or at least regulate it? Or is the state interfering in a private matter?

In sum, our examination shows quite a few things wrong with each of the above positions, and at first sight appears unproductive. Most of the positions are incomplete; they speak largely to the condition of only one party to the abortion activity. Some, moreover, contain considerations that are patently irrelevant—for instance, the claim that the Supreme Court reached its decision by bowing to pressure. Some are so emotion-charged that they hinder rather than contribute to clear thinking. Some allege empirical consequences that are so highly improbable as to merit no serious attention. The result of all this seems to be that we have been brought no nearer a final resolution.

Or have we? On second thought, something has been gained. We have been exposed to the range of considerations deserving attention. Certain bad arguments have been thrown out, which at least lets us see better what the problem is and clarifies what has to be done. Our investigation makes clear the necessity for giving systematic, measured attention to both parties, to their rights and freedoms. For "right" and "liberty" are at stake on both sides of the problem. And this entails going back to beginnings and asking what we mean by "right" and "liberty."

III. Some Underlying Concepts

A. *Liberty*

1. *Conceptualization*

While the concepts of "right" and "liberty" are closely related, they are not the same. "Right" is a strictly legal concept. Not so with "liberty"; it is a concept concerned with actual conditions.

The common dictionary notion behind "liberty" and its near-synonym "freedom" is that of doing as one pleases and, alternately, being unrestrained by others in doing so. This, by the way, is the meaning given the term by one of England's greatest philosophers, Thomas Hobbes, who said, "liberty properly signifieth the absence of opposition or impediment." The reference is to the realm of actuality, with the accent on the negative—the absence of restraint. Freedom of speech, one particular activity, means speaking as one wishes without human interference. Freedom in the large, in respect to all activities in which one engages, means acting as one wishes without human interference.

Manifestly, one and the same person can be free with respect to one activity (e.g., delivering a political oration) and unfree with respect to another (using foul and obscene language). One may be free with respect to one set of persons (not interfered with by the police, when delivering a political oration) and unfree with respect to another (harassed by a group of dissidents). The restraint marking lack of freedom may be psychological as well as physical; interference may take the form of disapproval as well as a physical barrier.

Diagram 2
LIBERTY: WANTS AND IMPEDIMENTS
Figure 1–4

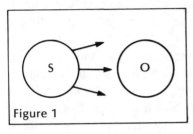

Figure 1

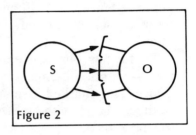

Figure 2

S = Self
O = Other

Arrow indicates WANTS or desire to carry on some activity.
Shield indicates IMPEDIMENTS to activity.

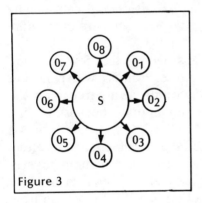

Figure 3

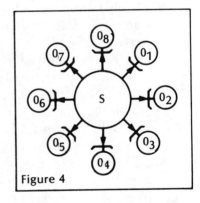

Figure 4

Finally, it follows from the definition, as an inescapable deduction, that freedom is tied to wants. A person who wants nothing cannot be unfree, for there is nothing he or she wants to do that may be interfered with. Correlatively, a person engaged in fulfilling wants should expect some interference (hence unfreedom), the degree varying with the number of such wants.

To further our conceptualization, these two opposing ideas—wants and impediments—are pictured in Diagram 2. The circles marked S mean self; those with O mean an "other." Lines with arrows at their heads depict the desire to carry on some activity; lines with T's at their heads represent shields or impediments to this activity. Self in Fig. 1 meets no impediments from the other person; self is thus "free" with respect to the other. Meeting impediments in Fig. 2, self is not free with respect to the other person. Fig. 3, then, depicts the completely free individual and Fig. 4, a completely unfree individual. By extension, one can imagine diagrams of the intermediate states between perfect freedom and perfect unfreedom.

Applying these considerations, we see that few of us are either totally free or totally unfree. Rather, we spend our lives oscillating, at times having wants we are free to pursue and at times having wants we cannot pursue because we find others blocking the way.

So far I have said nothing about government and its effect on liberty, and with good reason. For even without government there are infringements on liberty. Government or no government, there may be occasions when I stop you from doing what you want to do, or vice versa. And what effect does government have on liberty? If government does what on most theories it is supposed to do (namely, attempt to eradicate or reduce the more aggressive acts against person and property, such as killing, stealing, and raping), the effect is mixed. On the one hand, in thwarting the would-be thief or murderer, government is taking away liberty (for we assume that in most cases the thief wants to steal, the murderer wants to kill). On the other hand, when we look at it from the point of view of the would-be victims, government is not only *not* taking away liberty but is enlarging it. This assumes that the would-be victims want to keep their money, want to keep their lives.

In sum, government, in enforcing laws against the actions of individuals, takes away some liberty but may also indirectly enlarge liberty. And from this it may follow that, while in some cases government operation does result in a net decrease in liberty, in other cases the opposite is true. Take a system of traffic lights, for example. Although one's movement is, in the short range, frustrated at times by red lights, the long-range effect of the system is to provide greater freedom of movement and freedom from being impeded by a collision.

It is a great credit to John Locke that he saw this and, seeing it, placed it at the very center of his theory. Though he spoke more often of "right" than "liberty," and defined "liberty" a bit more narrowly than we have, he was clear not only in visualizing the desired effect of government to be an increase of liberty, but in conceiving the major function of government to be the provision of such increase—or, in his terms, the protection of life, liberty, and property. And this conception of government is closely followed in the Declaration of Independence, the Constitution, *The Federalist* papers, and the other great documents and tracts of our early history.

A slight elaboration of our earlier figures should clarify this point (see Diagram 3). If we postulate that one of 0's wants is to do away with S (representing this with an arrow), if we represent officials of government as a triangle standing over the two (visualize this as a policeman if you will), and if we hypothesize a law against murder, then, to the extent this law is effectively enforced, government's action can be represented as erecting a new impediment to O's action or, alternately, strengthening the shield representing S's self-defense. And from this we can see that, although O's liberty

Diagram 3
GOVERNMENT'S ROLE IN PROTECTING LIBERTY

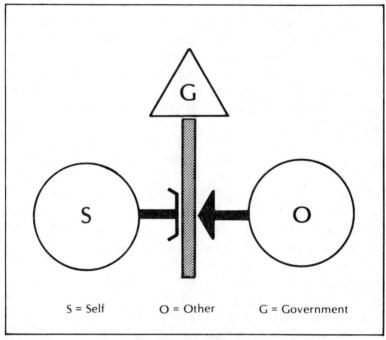

Other (O) wants to murder Self (S); self wants to protect self;
government enacts law against murder.

is further restricted, not only is S's liberty not restricted but
indirectly it is increased. For in safeguarding self's life,
government is protecting the *sine qua non* of one's doing
what one wants, which is life itself. Moreover, assuming that
most of the populace do not wish to be murdered, the net
effect of a law against murder is precisely what Locke
described it to be—an enlargement of liberty.

2. *Application*
Turning now back to the abortion issue, we can see how

inadequate it is to try to resolve it by referring simply to "liberty." In terms of liberty, from the woman's viewpoint, an abortion is the implementation of a wish to rid herself of an unwanted fetus, and she is free in this to the extent that she is not impeded. From the fetus's viewpoint, if we can so speak, it is quite the opposite. Freedom for it, the carrying out of its wants (assuming we can also use this phrase), is a matter of continuing to live and grow in the womb, un-harmed; and an abortion, by virtue of frustrating this want, is a denial of freedom. We have, in other words, a conflict of wants and, as a result, a conflict of freedoms. By simple extension of reasoning, a law prohibiting abortion reduces the woman's freedom, but increases that of the fetus. With or without governmental action, it is a case of liberty against liberty and therefore a matter no simple appeal to liberty can decide.[12]

B. *Right*

1. *Definition*

A "right" is defined here as "any power or privilege vested in a person by law or custom." To have a "right" to do something is to enjoy the protection of some recognized body of law or custom in doing it. To have a "right" to speak

---

12. The above analysis assumes the common-sense, want-oriented meaning of liberty. Other definitions lead to different results. Among these are the definitions that see liberty as doing without impediment not anything you *want,* but what you *ought* to do (Plato, church authorities) or what you want within certain limits of the law of nature (Locke). These definitions are tied to ethical norms. If the norm prohibits your committing a certain act (such as theft), then the placing of impediments in the way is not a deprivation of liberty. And the enjoyment of liberty is consistent with a considerable amount of restraint. And so, if killing the fetus be considered murder, on such definition not only would life indirectly be preserved through laws against abortion, but liberty too—including, particularly, the liberty of the prospective mother—would be indirectly preserved.

Also to be noted is that point of view which defines liberty as the absence simply of *governmental* restraint. On this view liberty and governmental action are mutually exclusive, and the prohibition of abortion would by definition be an abridgment of freedom.

your mind is to have a just claim to speak your mind, and demonstrating a just claim is a matter of pointing to an authoritative document (like the Constitution or the Bill of Rights) that contains a right of free speech. "Right" therefore refers to the realm of law, of norms and oughts, while "liberty" refers to the realm of fact, of history. "Right" is substantiated by pointing to an authoritative document; "liberty" to actual experience. For example, a "right" to worship as one pleases can be proved by citing a freedom-of-religion clause in an authoritative document; "liberty" to worship is proved by showing that people so doing are in fact not interfered with.

A "right" is a particular liberty protected by some law, and what applied to liberties applies also to rights. For rights also clash (such as a person's right to a fair trial versus a newspaper's right to freedom of the press). Government action should on balance protect rights, and government's major task should be, as our tradition holds, to "secure . . . rights." The problem where rights are concerned is the problem of identification—identification depending not upon a particular want (as in the case of liberty) but upon recognition by some authorative source.

2. Application

Where abortion is concerned, then, the first question accordingly is whether or not we can find in some authoritative document anything that explicitly or implicitly affirms the right of a fetus to continue growing in the womb, or the right of the woman to abort. Two of the gentlemen quoted in the first part of this chapter (authors of Statements #1 and #6) believe there is a "constitutional guarantee of the right to life" and an "unalienable right to life" on which the United States is founded; while a third (author of #3) suggests there is a right to life tied to an "absolute value of each human being." Two others (authors of #2 and #5) refer to a "right to privacy" and a "constitutional right of free choice in abortion." A third (author of #4) refers to unspecified "rights of the mother."

How stands the matter? Let us look at three of the most authoritative writings for American political society—the Constitution (including the Bill of Rights), the Declaration of Independence, and the political theory of John Locke. The Constitution, where it speaks of "rights" or their equivalent, speaks of life and liberty in one special context only, and in qualified terms at that; namely, one has the right not to have life and liberty taken away by state government "without due process of law" (Amendments Five and Fourteen), Thus the right to life and liberty, far from being an unqualified substantive matter, is on strict interpretation only a qualified procedural one. And the Constitution makes no reference to a right of abortion.

A look at the Declaration is more productive. For, as we all know, the first of the truths declared to be self-evident is that "all men are created equal"; the second, "that they are endowed by their Creator with certain unalienable rights," that is to say, rights that cannot be given away; and the third, "that among these are Life, Liberty, and the Pursuit of Happiness." The Declaration therefore proclaims the right of Life, from which we can infer the right of a fetus (if considered a person) not to be killed; and yet it also affirms the rights of Liberty and the Pursuit of Happiness, from which we can infer the right of a woman to manage what is hers as she sees most conducive to her happiness.

Finally, John Locke's *Second Treatise* contains an account of the origin and scope of authority of the legitimate state upon which the aforementioned rights rest. In Locke, heavy emphasis lies on the belief that the purpose of government is to protect the rights (Locke called them liberties) that people enjoy in the "state of nature," which precedes the establishment of government. These rights (called "natural rights" by others) are rights implied by a code of conduct for people in their dealings with one another, presumably written into the nature of the universe or handed down by God, and known as the law of nature. Locke did not undertake to specify in detail just what was included in this code. But the right to the enjoyment of what was one's own—what was "properly" the individual's—was central; and for what was one's own, Locke sometimes used the phrase "life, liberty, or estate" and sometimes the single term "property." One could do what one wished with one's own life, liberty, and property without legitimate interference from others, with the single qualification that it be "within the law of nature," which in practical terms meant as long as one did not encroach upon the life, liberty, and property of another.

Those who argue from "rights" therefore have something on their side. Although (Cardinal Krol in Statement #1 to the contrary) the Constitution says nothing explicitly about a "right to life," the Declaration and Locke do contain statements of the unalienable right to life. But on the other hand, there is also a general right to liberty, property, and the pursuit of happiness from which a right to abort might be reasonably deduced. Thus one finds conflicting rights. And although one may infer (by virtue of priority of statement, greater specificity, and logic) that the right to life is to be considered the more important, no rule is provided for resolving such conflict. And so we scarcely get beyond a standoff between the right of the fetus not be killed (if we can speak of the fetus as having rights) and the right of the woman to manage what is properly hers.

C. *Status of the Fetus*

So far we have been treating prospective mother and fetus as we would two persons, separate but equal, but modifying the comparison with an occasional phrase like "if we can speak of a fetus having rights." It is now time to face the root issue to which these remarks indirectly call attention, an issue of conceptualization at least as fundamental as that of the meaning of "liberty" and "rights," namely, the issue of whether or not the fetus is indeed to be treated as having coordinate status with the prospective mother.

The opposing viewpoints here should be reasonably clear from the position statements at the beginning of the chapter. Some, like the writers of Statements #3 and #6, see the fetus as a human being—not fully formed, to be sure, but alive and bearing the marks distinctive of homo sapiens even at an early stage. Abortion is in this view a matter of killing a human being, and hence the equivalent to manslaughter or murder. Others, like the authors of Statements #4 and #8, see the fetus as part of the woman's body—living tissue and potential life, but not actual life; a form of life that is dependent on the woman and that cannot subsist by itself. Abortion therefore is a matter of removing from the woman something that belongs to her and of which she wants to be rid.

Which group is right? The answer, to a certain extent, is both. For here we are in the presence of what some might call a paradox. It is hard, on one hand, to deny the contention of the first group that the fetus can be called at least the early stage of a human being, that in aborting it we are extinguishing a form of life, and that removing it from the womb is a much more serious matter than removing one's appendix. But it is equally hard to deny that the fetus is not a fully developed, independent, human being, or to deny that in aborting it we are removing what can in a valid sense be said to "belong" to the woman.

Thus, it is possible to see the fetus either as having equal status to the woman or as having unequal and subordinate status. Psychologists stress the point that certain impressions received by the mind may be quite as legitimately organized one way as another. To illustrate this they provide us with the famous picture (Fig. 1) that can be seen as either two faces or a single vase. Similarly, mother and fetus can be seen as either two people or one.

And yet, there is a difference. Though one may legitimately speak of both as forms of human life, the woman

Fig. 1
ALTERNATE PERCEPTIONS

Vase or Faces

(without whom the nonviable fetus cannot survive) is *more* of a human being than the fetus (without whom the woman can survive). Hence the depriving of the "life" of a fetus is of an order quite different from the killing of a child, spouse, or other person. And the social consequences pose far less of a danger than does a murderer loose in the neighborhood.

The answer to the question of when life begins is similarly ambiguous. One has hardly to examine in any depth the various positions on this issue to learn that the development of this condition we call "life" presents a continuum of gradual change from the manufacture of sperm and ova in the parents to the appearance of the offspring. To be sure some points in the process stand out more sharply than others, notably conception, "quickening" (moment of the first recognizable movement of the fetus in utero), "viability" (moment when the fetus is first capable of living outside the womb), and birth. But among these it seems dogmatic to elevate one to the position of primacy, as the beginning.

IV. THE SUPREME COURT OPINION

Granted that the Constitution, the most authoritative of our documents, treats the right to life and liberty only in general and highly qualified terms, may there not be more specific rights derivable by implication? And could not these include either a right to life on the part of the fetus (interpretable as a right not to be aborted) or a right of the prospective mother to her own body (interpretable to include a right to abort), or both? The answer is yes to the first question: such rights may be so derived. Let us now consider which rights have in fact been derived and how.

The Supreme Court, in the celebrated case of *Roe* v. *Wade*,[13] decided that a woman has a constitutional right to privacy that includes an unqualified right to terminate her pregnancy during the first trimester, though that right is qualified thereafter. The obverse of this decision is that no state can under our Constitution prohibit abortion during the first trimester, though states may regulate it for the sake of the woman's health in the second, and prohibit it in the third (save where necessary for the preservation of the life of the woman).

A. *History of the Legal Status of Abortion*

How did the Court reach this decision? In arguing its case, the Court first reviewed the history of the legal status of abortion, pointing out that neither the practice of the past nor the great political and legal philosophies of the past (the Stoics, Augustine, St. Thomas, and others), nor English common law or statute law, not even American statute law up to the latter half of the nineteenth century, had considered abortion before "quickening" a crime (quickening being placed at various points in midpregnancy, but normally in the fourth month). In other words, the Court noted, making abortion criminal in the first trimester dates only from the late nineteenth century. Before that time, a woman enjoyed a substantially broader right to terminate a pregnancy than she did under most state statutes in force at the time of the Court's deliberation. The Court further noted that a trend

---

13. January 22, 1973.

toward liberalization began in the 1950s and that certain quasi-public authorities, which had at one time supported the prohibition (the American Medical Association, the American Public Health Association, and the American Bar Association) reversed their views. And it further noted that one of the important reasons for this return to the classical liberal position was that the danger even early abortions had posed to a pregnant woman's life (which had been a leading reason for the move toward the restrictiveness of the nineteenth century) had been eliminated.

B. *Right of Privacy*

Having made these prefatory remarks, the Court turned to the central issue. It said first that a right of privacy is not explicitly found in the Constitution. But it then went on to argue that the roots of such a right are found in the Bill of Rights (a sort of "penumbra" of the particular rights there enumerated) and as part of the general concept of liberty, which is protected by the due process clause of the Fourteenth Amendment against any infringement by the state. While only such personal rights as can be deemed "fundamental" or "implicit in the concept of ordered liberty" are included in this right of privacy, earlier decisions made it clear that the right has some extension to marriage, procreation, and contraception. The Court concluded this right is broad enough to "encompass a woman's decision to terminate her pregnancy." Supporting the conclusion is the observation that state denial of this choice to a woman may do her much harm, both psychological and physical.

But this right of privacy is not absolute. The court was not agreeing with those who argue for a woman's "unlimited right to do with her body as she pleases." It said the right may be limited by the state, though only by a "compelling state interest." And it said the state may constitutionally find such an interest at later stages of pregnancy (the second two trimesters) in the form of an interest in protecting the woman's health and (the third trimester) protecting the potential life of the fetus. But for the first three months the woman's right to terminate her pregnancy, and the general right of privacy of which this is part, is unqualified, overriding contrary interests.

C. *The Fetus and Its Rights*

The Court then addressed the problem of the fetus and its rights. The form in which the Court raised the question was that of whether a fetus was a "person." It did this because if a fetus were a "person," then the prohibition of the Fourteenth Amendment forbidding a state to "deprive any person of life" without due process of law would apply; the fetus' life would be constitutionally protected against state action, and this would presumably require the state positively to protect that life. But the Court held that the fetus is not a person. And it did this on several grounds: first, in the Constitution the word "person" is used only in a post-natal meaning; second, the circumstances at the time of the passage of the Fourteenth Amendment (notably the far freer practices concerning abortion) were such as to suggest the term as used in the amendment did not include the unborn; and third, no case could be found where a fetus was considered a person.

But though not a person, and therefore not entitled to the protection of the Fourteenth Amendment, may not the fetus be considered a living being? The Court said that the question of when life begins is a difficult one, that those trained in medicine, philosophy, and theology have been unable to reach a consensus, and that the judiciary was not in a position to speculate upon it. Yet the Court strongly suggested that while there were those (notably Catholic officialdom since the nineteenth century, plus many non-Catholic individuals) who placed the beginning of life at conception, there were more numerous and prominent au-

thorities who placed it later.[14] And the Court pointed out
that, in areas other than criminal abortion, the law has been
reluctant to endorse any theory that life begins before live
birth.

In sum, the Court decided that the fetus does not have the
same human status as the pregnant woman, though as a
living embryo and potential human being the state has an
interest in protecting it. This interest increases as pregnancy
progresses until, at the point of "viability" (some time
between the twenty-fourth and twenty-eighth week), it becomes "compelling," entitling the state not only to regulate
but, in its discretion, even to override the woman's right and
to prohibit abortion.

D. *Summary*

Where rights are concerned, the Supreme Court's celebrated decision voices the view that:
1. The woman has a right to terminate pregnancy, a right
   derived from the Fourteenth Amendment.
2. The fetus does *not* have a right to life—not because
   such right is not found (such a right may also be derived
   from the Fourteenth Amendment), but because the
   fetus is not a person.
3. Hence, between woman and fetus, the woman's right
   to life prevails at all times during pregnancy.
4. The state, however, also has a right—rather, an
   authority—to protect the woman's life and health and
   the life or potential life represented by the unborn.
5. This right of the state grows as pregnancy progresses.
6. The woman's right to privacy takes precedence over
   the state's authority in the first trimester.
7. The state's authority takes precedence over the woman's right to privacy in the last trimester.

14. It has been placed at live births by the Stoics, most of Jewry, a large
segment of Protestants, some physicians; at quickening by common law
and Catholic officialdom from the Middle Ages until the nineteenth
century; and at viability by physicians increasingly today.

E. *Further Reflection*

There is a tendency to see the Court's conclusion as an authoritative resolution of the abortion matter that ought to conclude our opinions as lay persons. But there is still more to consider. The Court's decision is, to be sure, in one sense authoritative (the Court being the final interpreter of the meaning of the Constitution and its decisions placing legal limits on state power), but to accept the Court's reasoning is another matter. Its decision can and should conclude our action but not our thought. Where thought is concerned, the Court merely presents a reasoned argument, noť, by the way, on the main issue of whether government prohibition of abortion is or is not "good," but only on the lesser issue of whether our national Constitution prohibits our state governments from prohibiting abortions. And how well or poorly reasoned the Court's argument is—how strong the premises, how straight the logic—on this you and I have the right to judge.

Is the Court's position in the abortion case well argued? Several respected leaders think not, seeing it as poor law. First, they claim that pointing to the long historical survey of the legal status of abortion is tantamount to saying, "One reason we think the Constitution prohibits a state from banning abortion is that in our legal and philosophic history the act was rarely viewed as "criminal"—reasoning which you and I are entitled to question.

But the strongest grounds for questioning the Court's activity in measuring constitutionality are: (1) the nature of the process of deliberation itself (one considerably less objective than an engineer's activity in measuring the strength of steel, and of necessity one containing a measure of "subjectivity") and (2) the fact that the Justices themselves often disagree. They disagree sometimes on conclusions, sometimes on reasoning, sometimes on both. They even disagree at times on the interpretation of a case they severally decided in the past, and on its relevance to the one

currently under scrutiny. In the abortion case, Justices
Rehnquist and White took issue with the majority—the
latter, strong issue.

Justice White saw the majority view as saying that the
Constitution values the convenience or whim of the woman
in the time before viability more than the life or potential life
of the fetus. He claimed that the Constitution was therefore
being interpreted as guaranteeing "the mother's right to an
abortion as against any state law seeking to protect the fetus
from an abortion not prompted by more compelling reasons
of the mother." He then expressed his dissent. He found
"nothing in the language or history of the Constitution to
support the Court's judgment." And he accordingly accused
the Court of simply fashioning a new constitutional right for
pregnant women "with scarcely any reason or authority,"
investing that right with sufficient substance to override
most existing state abortion statutes. And so, said Justice
White, the people of the states are constitutionally kept from
weighing the relative importance of the continued existence
of the fetus, on the one hand, against a spectrum of possible
impacts on the woman, on the other. The main point, he
concluded, is that regardless of whether or not he or anyone
else "might agree with [the Court's] marshalling of values,"
he saw no constitutional warrant for imposing such an order
of priorities on the people and legislatures of the states.

Seven justices find a "right to privacy" in the Constitution; two do not. Under these circumstances, it is clear that
we lay persons not only have no duty to accept the Court's
thinking (although we are bound by its legal decision), but
each of us must come to his or her own conclusion.

V. SYNTHESIS

The burden of these inquiries into basic concepts and the
Court's decision is that "intelligent reflection" on the abortion activity can lead to two quite different outcomes. How

does this come about? This can best be answered by delineating the trains of thought of tow hypothetical thinkers, Citizen X and Citizen Y.

Citizen X reflects that the issue at bottom resolves itself into two subissues: first, the balance between the rights, liberties, and interests respectively of fetus and woman, and second, the question of the authority of the state. As to the first, it seems to him that the interests of the fetus ought to take precedence. For the fetus, undeveloped as it is, is nevertheless a form of a human being, and its claim to life surely is weightier than the woman's claim to relief from the burden of childrearing. The woman is not without other recourse; she may put the child up for adoption. And evidence of the deleterious effects of having an unwanted child does not clearly outweigh that of the deleterious effects of an abortion upon the woman. As to the second subissue (the authority of the state), it seems to Citizen X there can be no question; the protection of the life of an individual, especially in a country professing the philosophy of John Locke, is acknowledgedly not only within the confines of the state but is its very raison d'être. And if the actual power of the state has been deficient, as it has, with abortions taking place illegally, surely the remedy is the providing of more resources and stronger laws.

Citizen Y, on the other hand, while analyzing the problem in the same way, nevertheless resolves oppositely the critical subissues. He sees the fetus in the first trimester not as a human being but only as potential life, and thus clearly secondary to the woman. Even if one should accept the argument that the fetus is a form of a human being, it is nevertheless different from the woman; it is a human being *in potentia,* dependent upon the woman in the close sense that the woman is not dependent upon it. The fetus is part of the woman as the woman is not part of it. The woman's aborting it is the removal from her body of something belonging to her—of something that cannot exist without her—and her claim to this liberty is not unjustly considered superior to any claim the fetus might have to life. As for the authority of the state, it seems to Citizen Y that the presumption is always against state intervention (reasoning with Locke that government is the fiduciary of the people), and this presumption should be sustained in a dispute involving two parties where one party can justly be considered part of, the property of, the other.

Both of these positions are dispassionate and comprehensive, taking into account both parties to the abortion act, their respective rights and freedoms, as well as the authority of government. Both are reasonable positions, the philosophical arguments thus ending up pretty much a draw.

*   *   *

So far we have considered (1) the rights and wrongs of the abortion act and the impact of the activity on society (what I call the "social issue") and (2) the authority of the state to intervene (what I call the "political issue"). But there are further considerations to the political issue than the authority of the state. We must look at the impact of government intervention on society as a whole.

First of all, to justify intervention, one must not only see the activity in question as bad but also see the chances of government's controlling the activity as reasonably good. This latter is, in turn, a matter partly of practicality and partly of the existence of a supporting consensus. In the abortion case government control of the activity is neither practical nor supported by a consensus. It is not practical since many women seek abortions regardless of legality, and in so doing, they risk great danger to their health and lives. It is not supported by a consensus, as polls show that the majority of Americans believe in choice. Thus, even if there were general accord on the immorality of the abortion act, the problem of unenforceability and the consequent danger to the uncomplying woman are so great that it would not be in the interest of society for the state to intervene.

A second consideration, in this controversy where the two sides (using the same process of rational thought but starting with different premises) reach opposite conclusions on the social issue, is the impact of government intervention on the rights of the two sides as protected by the First Amendment. Since the starting premises reflect different moral/religious beliefs, we must ask if government intervention would restrict the rights of either group to exercise its beliefs. And we find it would. For government prohibition of abortion takes away the liberty of those who believe in choice to have an abortion in a legal and safe way, while the lack of government intervention does not restrict the liberty of those opposed to continue with pregnancy. Or to put it another way, government intervention forces the values of one group on the other, while the absence of government intervention gives each group the freedom to live according to its own values. And once again we must return to Locke and his presumption against government intervention.

$$* \quad * \quad *$$

There are several important implications of the foregoing discussion. First, intelligent reflection on *the abortion activity* (the social issue) may at times lead as reasonably to one conclusion as to another—may equally, or almost equally, support opposite findings. For one may as legitimately choose one starting point as another (define human being to include or to exclude the fetus), as validly strike one particular balance as another (treat the life of the fetus as more than or less than the liberty of the mother), and from this as rightly resolve the initial question of the propriety of the activity one way as another.

A second implication, a most important one, is that even if abortion is considered wrong or evil, intelligent reflection on *government intervention* (the political issue) does not necessarily compel the conclusion that the state should intervene.

Quite the contrary, the benefits or drawbacks of the political question must be judged separately from the merits or evils of the activity.

Finally, it is important to remember that no position—not even the strongest, the most perfect—is beyond legitimate challenge. None is without some element of uncertainty. For the facts relevant to the problem are never finally determined.

VI. CONCLUSION: GOVERNMENT AND LIBERTY

Our case study, the controversy over abortion, has a number of broad implications for general problems involving government and liberty—for the nature of those problems, for the method of attacking them, and for their resolution.

As to the *nature of the problem,* given the common sense definition of liberty (doing what one wants without impediment), it should be noted first that most such problems involve a conflict of liberties from the very start, before one even considers government intervention; hence to decide the problem it is insufficient to appeal to liberty alone. The same is true with rights, for it is the uncommon case when the appeal of one party to "right" is clearly stronger than the other's. Thus the problem initially starts with a conflict of values.

It should be noted second that even where, in its initial form, the problem is readily resolvable (for example, by showing that one person's liberty or rights are more justified than the other's), it may not be so readily resolvable when the impact of government intervention is taken into account. For government intervention by definition is some infringement of liberty and very possibly of rights, too. And such infringement may outweigh the infringement existing in government's absence; in other words, the cure may be worse than the disease. Or intervention may be ineffective, produce a new crop of ills, and compromise other values, as has been in some degree the case with antiabortion laws, with their by-product of disrespect for laws, injury to health, and even threat to life—all occasioned by illegal abortions.

The supposition that having decided the activity in question is "bad," one is automatically entitled to conclude that state prohibition is "good" is one of the more common mistakes that people make when confronting problems of government and liberty—or, for that matter, other problems involving government. Anyone who is inclined to invoke governmental authority should always do two things: (1) weigh the conflicting liberties and values and (2) ask whether government intervention is, all things considered, effective and right.

As to *method,* the procedure for intelligent reflection on social activity, as I see it, is this: (1) break down an issue into its constituent elements, specifying alternative actions and the opposing values, and then make the connections between the two; (2) test these connections against the criteria of intuitive, existential, or rational truth, and (3) aggregate results through a process of weighing and balancing. Intelligent reflection on political issues is a matter of subjecting the actions or proposed actions of government (notably but not exclusively those of legislative character) to this same process. The accent is on completeness, balance, accuracy in testing, sobriety, and a certain temperance, which acknowledges the impossibility of reaching perfect judgments.

Finally, as to the *resolution* of these problems—the product of intelligent reflection—any rational conclusion we come up with will not necessarily point a single way only, and it must always include an element of the tentative. Minds, equally careful in their workings, can at times come to opposite but equally sound conclusions. These conclusions are virtually bound to have an element of the conditional about them, such as the circumstances when abortion should be permitted or not permitted. And tentativeness may even persist when rational thought points heavily in one direction. For, as the abortion issue illustrates, the axioms or definitions that constitute starting points of intelligent reflection may legitimately differ, and some of the contentions that necessarily enter into calculations (e.g., amount of mental distress) cannot be completely tested.

Chapter IV
Government and Equality: Discrimination in Employment

Another issue citizens have to confront in assessing the activities of government centers on that relationship of human to human called equality. This relationship may be connected to the organization of government in a number of ways. Equality may be a principle for taking part in the structuring of government, in the very setting up of the system itself, or in the filling of offices thus set up. It may be a principle behind the rules for reaching decisions in the legislative branch or a guide for applying and implementing the decisions reached. And it may be an objective of government.

In our own scheme of government, equality comes into the picture at all these points. The suffrage is to be universal among adults and equally distributed—one person, one vote. Members of the legislature are to make their decisions on the same principle. Citizens are to enjoy the equal protection of the law. And equality may be said to enter into the aims of our government, since one of the objectives of the Constitution is the establishment of justice—meting out rewards and punishments equitably.

In the last few years equality has entered the political picture in a new context. There has been an increasingly insistent demand that people in their public dealings with one another serve, hire, rent to, and admit equally—a demand that first government itself do so; then railroads, restaurants, and other concerns affected with a public interest; then schools; and, more recently, employers and landlords. And this demand has been supplemented by a second one: that government see to it that this be done.

In relation to employment, the demand is that organizations not discriminate between individuals for *irrelevant reasons,* that is, for reasons not connected with performance on the job. Responsive to these demands, our national, state, and local governments have enacted antidiscrimination legislation and set up enforcement agencies (such as the Equal Employment Opportunity Commission of the federal government) charged with seeing that members of certain groups (minorities and women) not be denied jobs on account of such membership.

The object of this chapter is to assess the reasoning behind extending this principle still further, and to do this we will look at a controversy over gay rights in Boulder, Colorado. The specific details apply to only one city, but similar controversies, involving most of the same concepts, have arisen in many other parts of the country.

I. The Case:
Sexual Preference Ordinance

In December, 1973, an ordinance was introduced in the Boulder City Council to amend the chapter in the City Code entitled "Discrimination in Housing, Employment, and Public Accommodation Unlawful." The proposed amendment, which became known as the "sexual preference ordinance," prohibited discrimination in employment on account of sexual preference, a phrase it defined as "an inclination or preference for or an orientation towards intimate sexual relations with a member of one's own sex or with members of both sexes." More precisely, it sought to bring to bear the coercive power of government against employers who refused to hire or who chose to fire on grounds of sexual preference. The acknowledged aim was to extend the protection accorded blacks, Hispanics, women, and other minorities or quasi-minorities to homosexuals (gays and lesbians).[1] The acknowledged premise was that this minority was in fact a victim of prejudice in employment and was in fact being hired or fired on grounds irrelevant to competence in job performance.

The sexual preference ordinance became the center of an increasingly stormy debate and controversy for five months before it finally was laid to rest by voter rejection in a popular referendum. Initiated by the mayor (a black) and seconded by a youthful councilman who generally was considered the representative of the university students, the ordinance was supported by the three women on the nine-member council and also by the Boulder Human Rights Commission. In the community at large, support came from various groups representative of minorities and liberal perspectives, such as the National Organization for Women, a large section of the University of Colorado (student body and faculty alike), and, naturally, the various homosexual groups. The ordinance was opposed by the remaining four members of the council (all white business or professional men) and, in the community at large, by business groups like the Chamber of Commerce, by certain church groups, and by another but apparently much smaller section of the university. The two sides vied with each other in presenting their cases to the council at public hearings, and to the community at large, through the organization of special ad hoc groups and through a steady stream of letters-to-the-editor and advertisements in the press.

The ordinance's career through the city council reflected the growing turbulence. It was given a quiet first reading on December 18 and was routinely passed, with no dissent. But

1. To avoid repeatedly using the awkward phrase "gays and lesbians," and since there is no agreed-upon comprehensive term, I will use the word "gay" to mean both homosexual men and women, as it was used at the time of the controversy.

as the opposition became aware of its substance and apparent implications, pressure mounted for postponement of the second reading. This was put off a number of times. Finally, a special public hearing was held, which took on the character of high drama and led one reporter to liken it to "the greatest show on earth." The second reading was further postponed as weeks of heated debate and emotional outbursts from all parts of the community ensued. Finally, on March 5, the ordinance passed by a bare 5-4 margin. But by this time the community had become so badly split that the council, under the mayor's leadership, decided to hold off enactment until the matter could be referred to the people. On this referendum, held on May 7, 1974, the measure lost heavily, by a 2 to 1 margin. Yet the matter did not end there. The opponents then sought recall of the original sponsors, and only after a recall election was held the following July (in which the mayor was retained and the youthful councilman removed) was the episode properly closed.

II. General Arguments

The sexual preference debate filled the pages of the city's press in steady crescendo for nearly half a year and, while highly varied in the number, kinds, and quality of arguments, nonetheless featured several insistent themes on each side.

At the most general level, supporters of the ordinance presented it as a "meaningful extension of human freedom," a step in the "ongoing struggle for human rights and human dignity," and a case of righting an "obvious wrong." They drew on the authority of Thomas Jefferson, the Declaration of Independence, and the Bill of Rights, deriving from the Declaration's rights to "life, liberty, and the pursuit of happiness" a specific right to gainful employment. Some claimed the authority of Christianity and its alleged abhorrence of discrimination. Others relied on the analogy to discrimination on account of race and sex, asking in effect why, if restrictions on employers in these cases were acceptable, the same should not be true for homosexuals. And one person went so far as to allege that "unless all people's rights are guaranteed by law, all rights are jeopardized" and asked, "Who knows what group will be next?" Constantly reiterated was the theme that gays were "harassed and oppressed" because of the prejudice held against them and that they were being forced to conceal their true preferences in sexual matters.

Opponents of the ordinance took an entirely different view of the issue. Homosexuality was not simply one other among many life-styles. It was a "sexual aberration" or form of sickness, its practitioners "deviates." It was, moreover, condemned in the eyes of many as a "sin" against God's holy law, and the protection contemplated under the ordinance was seen as a violation of the freedom of religion tenet of the Bill of Rights. A second theme stressed the inconsistency of the ordinance with the right of employers to hire whom they would, a right they said was derived from the Declaration of Independence. A third line of attack dwelt upon the baleful effects of homosexuality: gays in the roles of teachers and youth directors were said to corrupt the young, spread venereal disease, and set fires. To pass the ordinance was not only to legislate immorality but to open the gates to similar legislation protective of such exotic subgroups, as people with red hair, brown eyes, or hair-partings on the left. It would have a secondary effect on businesses, particularly small businesses, in the form of discouragement of trade. Finally, it would, by a process of attraction, make Boulder a mecca for others of like sexual preference, turning the city into a "Lesbian Homoville." Opponents laid a particular emphasis on the failure of proponents to cite cases, pointing out that only one had been cited—that of a lesbian teacher who was said to have been forced to resign from the school district several years back.

Retorting, proponents found the anti-gay reaction "shocking," tantamount to "smear tactics." The ordinance was not a case of legislating morality, but of protecting rights. And rights, in the minds of some of the proponents, lay only on the gays' side; they saw references to the employer's right to hire as nothing more than a cover for prejudice and as "shocking" examples of "bigotry." The harm alleged to be done by gays was not proven. And, as for the lack of cases, the reply was, in effect, that numbers make no difference: even if there was only one person discriminated against on account of sexual preference, the evil was present nonetheless.

A. *The Affirmative Position*

Let us now narrow the focus and look closely at some of the more reasoned arguments put forth by the two sides, starting with the affirmative. Among prominent supporters of the ordinance were (1) the mayor, an attorney-at-law, and (2) the leader of the Gay Liberation group, a candidate for a doctorate in Economics at the University of Colorado. Summarizing their positions is somewhat risky, as this requires piecing together arguments from a variety of public statements, interviews, and guest editorials. But one can detect the following major strands of thought:

(1) *Gays in Boulder are being discriminated against in employment.* Although there was only one case cited (that of the school teacher) there were others in the community, but those involved were reluctant to speak out, lest this information ruin their lives. A recent survey had shown that 12 percent of Boulder's employers would fire an employee if that employee were discovered to be gay. And furthermore, the attitudes expressed at the public hearing demonstrated "actual and potential job discrimination."

(2) *The possibility of being discharged from their jobs creates an intense fear and anxiety in gay people.* The mayor said no one should have to live that way and he initiated the sexual preference ordinance in order to build a community "free from fear."

(3) *Discrimination violates basic human rights,* for gays share a right—derived directly from the rights of life, liberty, and the pursuit of happiness—"to earn a living," "to work," and "to survive." In short, the ordinance "preserves the *right to work* for people who are homosexual," so long as they do not let that status adversely affect their ability to do the job.

(4) *The rights involved on the employer's side count less heavily than those on the employee's,* because those of the employer attach only to property, not to persons. The employer's rights take precedence over the gay's right to earn a living only when the gay's presence confronts the businessperson with a clear danger of bankruptcy.

(5) *Gays constitute a legitimate minority,* not a visible minority like blacks but a minority that is nonetheless a "true" one.

(6) *The rights asked for homosexuals are only those already won by blacks, Hispanics, and other minorities.*

(7) *Government has an "affirmative duty" to "enforce the rights* of the minority" and to assure equal protection under the law.

(8) *Passage of the ordinance would put an end to an environment of prejudice* and build a true community dedicated to the "preservation and enhancement of human dignity of all people."

(9) *The ordinance would not "legislate morality" nor "condone homosexuality."*

B. *The Opposing Position*

Let us now turn to the more reasoned arguments put forth by the opponents of the ordinance. Among prominent opponents were (1) an attorney and ex-councilman who came to be the leader of the ad hoc group opposing the ordinance, and (2) the editorial staff of Boulder's leading newspaper, the *Daily Camera.* Again, one takes certain risks in summarizing their positions, but the major threads of their argument are as follows:

(1) *The proposed law would afford one group a protected or preferred status while restricting the rights or freedoms of another.*

(2) *The rights of life, liberty, and the pursuit of happiness that are involved here inure equally to both sides.* The amendment would "violate the fundamental right of every employer to choose the people who work with him according to his own standards and judgments, outside the classic and accepted areas of discrimination."

(3) *The constitutional amendments that speak of equal protection and due process* (Fifth and Fourteenth), rather than being intended to protect one individual from another, were *intended to protect the individual from government.* Therefore the only true constitutional issue involved here is whether a government action that would limit the guaranteed rights of one individual (the employer's right to hire and fire being a presumed property right) can be justified on the grounds of "a compelling state interest in curing or attempting to cure a significant social disorder." And this is not the case.

(4) *Not all discrimination is necessarily bad,* as is testified to by the fact the term "discriminating" has both positive and negative connotations; it is partially a matter of taste. The proposed ordinance would take government too far, for it would impose one group's tastes and preferences (the gay's) upon another's (the employer's). Seeing all discrimination as bad "can only lead to a society without tastes, without morals, without individualism—in short, a homogenized, pasteurized society of robots."

(5) *Seeing simple legal prohibition as a cure-all for social ills invites a great increase of legislation,* which, with

its attendant evil of lack of sufficient enforcement, may lead to a total breakdown of respect for law.

(6) *The ordinance is not necessary,* primarily because there are no documented cases of discrimination in employment on account of sexual orientation in this city. (The lesbian teacher was under the jurisdiction of the school district and taught outside the city limits.) And it is unnecessary because it already is legal in Colorado for consenting adults to engage in homo- sexuality in private. Homosexuals therefore already have equal protection in their legitimate constitutional rights.

(7) *The ordinance "would crystallize into law special recognition and privilege for a minority by choice."*

*   *   *

The above arguments, on both sides of the controversy, are reasonably systematic, reasonably well-put-together positions. All are based on judgments fitting in the various categories of value, fact, authority, and logic. There are appeals to goods and bads on both sides, including those "goods" protected by law, called rights. The pros appeal to the good of human dignity and the bad of irrelevant discrimi- nation in hiring, prejudice against unorthodox life-styles, and division in the community; the cons appeal to the good of diversity, discrimination in taste, and the right to choose one's associates, and to the bad of privileged position, excess of law, and disrespect for law. There are appeals to alleged facts on both sides: the pros point to the fear felt by homosexuals, the firing of the school teacher for her les- bianism, and the prospective lifting of that fear on passage of the ordinance; the cons point to the corruption of youth, the loss of business, the litigation, and overregulation that would take place in the event the ordinance should pass.

There are appeals to authority on both sides, both sides invoking the Declaration of Independence, the Constitution, and the Bill of Rights. And there are appeals to logic: deducing a right to nondiscrimination from the Declaration's rights to life, liberty, and the pursuit of happiness, and treating opposition to the ordinance as evidence of pervasive community discrimination in hiring. To probe the reasonableness of these various allegations is our next job.

III. CRITIQUE OF UNDERLYING CONCEPTS

Readers who followed the discussion of the abortion case will already be taking the preliminary steps in analysis there laid out and applying them to the case at hand. They will note first that what makes the controversy is a clash of wants and liberties. The gays want not to have their life-style count against them in employment. Employers want to retain the choice of whether or not to count that life-style in their decisions. Gays want to be unimpeded by employer choices in their search for employment; employers want to be unimpeded in their choices. Both appeal to opposite rights, which on their face appear equally valid. So we are deprived, at first look, of the possibility of deciding the matter by simple appeal to liberty or right. It is, at least, one freedom against another and possibly also one right against another.

The reader will note second that a new concept arises with this issue. The principal ground on which those supporting the sexual preference ordinance based their case was equality and equal treatment. The theme, sounded with increasing insistence as the controversy moved to its conclusion, was that of equal freedom, equal protection, or, to take the label that came to be attached to the ordinance, "gay equal rights." The core of the supporting argument was this: "Gays are being denied rights that others have and all are entitled to; they are being treated unequally and unfairly, with disastrous effects upon them and, indirectly, upon the community." The opposition challenged at each point.

To determine whether rights at all have been denied to

gays, we must first determine which rights, if any of those cited, have a legitimate claim. To determine need for government intervention, we must first determine whether or not there has been discrimination and, if so, to what extent. And since the equality element is at the core of the dispute, we must look at the basic concept before evaluating its application to employment opportunity for a specific minority group.

A. *Rights*

We confront first the question of rights. Note the number of rights claimed to be involved by the two sides, especially by the proponents. One finds on this side not only the familiar right to life, liberty, and the pursuit of happiness, but also the right to earn a living, right to work, right to live free from want, right to survive, and right to human dignity. On the other side one finds the right to property, the right to hire and fire, and the right to associate with whom one pleases.

To sort these out and determine relative validity, we have to go, as urged in the preceding chapter, to the most authoritative sources. These are the Declaration of Independence, with its celebrated trinity that the government is to secure, the Constitution of the United States (the most authoritative source), and the particular state constitution involved (here, Colorado). One looks here because, if an assertion of right is to mean anything legally and practically, (that is, if its protection is to be translated into concrete action), the person asserting it must be able to trace its existence to the documents that found and establish our political system.

What, more specifically, are these rights? Where the Declaration is concerned, the first two terms of the trinity, "life" and "liberty," come directly from John Locke, and the claim they constitute is quite simply the claim of one individual not to be harmed by another in his life, health, liberty, or possessions. I have the right not to be killed, maimed, or kidnapped, or to have my car destroyed by you. You for your part have the duty not to do these things to me. And these rights, these duties, are reciprocal. Within these limits, you and I have the liberty to do with our persons or possessions as we see fit. To secure these rights, to secure these limits is the function of government—and the sole function. As for the right to the "pursuit of happiness," which Jefferson substituted in the Declaration for " property," the right is to pursue, not to win or acquire or have or be given.

The Constitution, aside from the Thirteenth Amendment's protection against "involuntary servitude," refers to the basic *rights of man against man* only obliquely, in the Ninth Amendment. The rights it speaks about directly, largely those enumerated in the first eight amendments, are *rights of the individual against government*. And so are certain other rights derived by the Supreme Court from the Constitution. Some of these are substantive, protecting citizens in the normal course of their lives (freedom of speech, press, religion, and the rights to assemble and to bear arms). Some are procedural, offering citizens special protection when they are "proceeded against" for alleged offence against the law (not to be subjected to unreasonable search and seizure, not to be deprived of life and liberty without due process, not to be placed in double jeopardy, etc.). But all of these are rights *against government* rather than against persons. The major part of them in our national constitution lie against the federal government (Amendments One-Eight), although some (notably those of the first clause of the Fourteenth Amendment) lie against the state governments. And of these the right not to be deprived "of life, liberty, or property, without due process of law" has been expanded, in Court interpretation, so that it no longer is confined to procedural matters alone, but also embraces the substantive rights of the First Amendment. State constitutions follow much the same line, with protection extending only, of course, against the states.

The clear implication of the above is that there is very little justification for grounding the position of either side to the sexual preference dispute on "rights," taking "rights" in the hard, practical sense of something clearly anchored in fundamental law and so enforceable in the courts. This is particularly true of the affirmative position. If one seeks to deduce a right not-to-be-discriminated-against-in-employment from the right to liberty of the Declaration, as did the mayor and gay leader, one faces the difficulty that the claim as first asserted (by Locke) almost certainly was intended to protect only from the most spectacular and extreme and coarsest of inroads (viz, kidnapping, holding captive). Or, if one argues a wider meaning, one opens the way to an equal and opposite claim on the side of the employer. To deduce the right not-to-be-discriminated-against from the right to the "pursuit of happiness" is to mistake a right to the means for a right to the end. To derive it, as the gay leader does, from a "right to earn a living," of which there is no mention in any of our documents, and describe this as "the very right to life" (of the Declaration) is to play with words. So, less clearly, is talking about a right to survive. Our national constitution, as we have noted, with a minor exception, says nothing about the rights of one person against another. Nor does the Colorado constitution. At the core of the argument supporting the gay rights ordinance is a conception of right not merely as a negative claim but as a positive demand: a claim to be given help, a job.

The opponents fare better, even though their argument is not without contention. A right to hire and fire as one chooses without state interference can be derived from the constitutional imperative. It has been. For the Supreme Court, in enlarging the protection of the 14th Amendment against a state's depriving "a person of life, liberty, and property without due process," has given to "deprivation of property" a meaning large enough to encompass a right to hire and fire as one pleases. Yet there are difficulties here, beyond those that arise from the validity of the Court's reasoning in so extending the protection of the amendment. For the Court in a long line of cases has made clear that this right to hire or fire is not absolute: the right yields to the authority of the state to impose limits for a compelling general interest, such as health and safety, and specifically, to prevent discrimination on account of sex and race.

Where the matter of rights is concerned, there is a difference between this case and the abortion one of the preceding chapter. There, leaving aside for the moment the status of the fetus, there was reason for speaking of the fetus' right against the woman, its life being at stake, or even of the woman's right against the fetus, her liberty being in a fundamental sense at stake. There was reason for the fetus' claim on the state for protection, as for the woman's claim against state interference. Here, however, the strongest case for affirming "right" is that of the employer against the state. But as we have seen, even that right must be heavily qualified; for already the employer's right has been found to yield to a general interest in protecting certain groups from discrimination in employment.

B. *Extent of Discrimination*

We confront now the second point underlying the controversy: the extent of the existing inequality of treatment and hence the need for remedial action. Here we have an issue of fact, as against value, law, or reasoning. Normally citizens trying to make up their minds intelligently on an issue will find it difficult to obtain reliable data. In the present case, however, considerable information was available at or near the beginning of the controversy. The leader of the gay movement stated that gays had received no police harassment and that he knew of no employers who asked job applicants what their sexual preferences were, and he cited only one case of firing (the lesbian school teacher). He rested his case on the asserted and potential fear of discrimination and fear of loss of job. At the same time, another spokesman for the gays testified to their widespread employment and to the existence of data suggesting that five out of six employers do not discriminate. This is persuasive evidence that there was little actual discrimination and that the opposition was right in its contention of no need for legislative action.

* * *

The conclusion thus far is twofold. First, there is no general right that protects nongays but not gays. What clear-cut, determinate rights there are, such as freedom of speech and of the press, and freedom from arbitrary arrest and unreasonable search, gays already enjoy. There is also equal protection of the laws. But equal treatment in hiring and firing is not such a general right; and gays not being extended this treatment are not being deprived of a right.

Second, on the evidence of the gays themselves, actual discrimination (unequal treatment) is rather rare, certainly not widespread. If fear of it is common, and one accepts the group's judgment that it is, it is not founded on facts; it is based rather on the unknown reaction of the individual employer or potential employer.

But even if no right is in question, and the need is not overwhelming, it is still possible to argue that equity nevertheless requires intervention for two reasons: (1) though the hurt be small, though only one person live in fear, the state should step in, and (2) gays are entitled to the same protection afforded other minorities. To consider these new points is the subject of our next section, which starts with a consideration of the "equality" concept itself.

C. *Equality*

1. *The Concept.* As with liberty, equality is a relationship of human to human. Liberty, in its most general sense, is a matter of one person's doing something without interference from another. Equality, in its most general sense, is a matter of two persons being "exactly the same in measure, quan-

tity, number, or degree," of being "like in value, quality, status, or position." But as the general definition of liberty did not get us far, neither does that of equality; we need to particularize those attributes and conditions that the two persons are said to have or enjoy in exactly the same measure, quantity, number, or degree.

Historically, where political philosophy is concerned, primarily three senses of the term equality have been utilized. There is first the wholesale sense, as in the phrase, "All men are created equal." This affirms that all people are of the same value in the eyes of nature or God, that they enjoy the same unalienable rights. Equality or inequality can here be viewed as the relationship between the inner core (the indestructible essence of the total human personality) of one individual to that of another. This inner core is distinguished from the outer shell of human beings, which comes into play in the second sense of the meaning of equality.

This second sense is more particularized. It is the sense in the phrase, "Men are not equal in physical strength, intelligence, honesty, or beauty." Equality or nonequality can here be viewed as the relationship between elements of the outer shells of human beings. If we designate these respectively as the body (implying qualities like height, weight, shape, skin color), the mind (implying qualities like memory, verbal skill, mathematical skill, reasoning ability), and a less tangible entity called character or spirit (implying reliability, honesty, integrity, and so forth), then equality is the condition of two people having an equal amount or degree of one or more of these components.

There is a third specialized sense referring to particular institutional arrangements. Equality of voice or participation implies that two citizens have the same vote in government; inequality, that they do not, as was the case when only those of certain amounts of property, or only whites, or only males had the vote. Equality of protection, application, or treatment implies that two citizens are alike subject to the law, regardless of race, color, wealth, sex, and so forth; inequality, that they are not.

John Locke's *Second Treatise* and its intellectual descendent, our own Declaration of Independence, enshrine and sanctify certain of these meanings while ignoring others. Locke starts out by affirming the equality of individuals in the wholesale sense of being granted alike certain natural or prepolitical rights, and of being not predesignated by nature or God as ruler or ruled. This is what is meant by the Declaration's statement, "All men are created equal." Both Locke and the authors of the Declaration reject the notion, not uncommon in preceding political thought, that nature or God divinely appointed one or another family as ruler, hence consigning the rest of a society to being ruled. From Locke's initial proposition is derived the further one that individuals have an equal right to participate in the *forming of government*. Allied to these concepts is the still further one that all laws shall apply equally to all segments of the community; conversely, in Locke's words, there is not to be "one law for the rich, another for the poor."

Other familiar notions are not enshrined in the sacred documents. Individuals are not considered empirically equal in strength, skill, or mind; in fact, quite the contrary. Nor were they believed by Locke to be equally entitled to participate in the *operation of the government*. Though the *Second Treatise* and the Declaration do not exclude the possibility of democracy, they do not specifically require it. Rather, they left open the question of how broadly, or how narrowly, the suffrage was to be distributed—the unwritten expectation being, however, that restricted patterns would prevail, with suffrage and office-holding being limited to those of certain families and of certain amounts of property in Locke's case, and to those of certain amounts of property in the case of the Declaration.

This disgression into the past is made in order to narrow down the issue that confronts us today. Equality in the wholesale, normative sense is no longer in dispute. Because our prevailing political philosophy is Lockean and Jeffersonian, few seriously question that we are created equal in the broadest, metaphysical sense, that we are equally worthy in the sight of God. Few seriously question the moral imperative derived from this, that we ought to treat one another as alike entitled to life and liberty, in the most fundamental sense. Few dispute that all alike should be entitled to vote and hold office, that restrictions on grounds of sex or color are wrong. People long ago stopped questioning whether the law should apply alike to rich and poor, black and white. But the issue that confronts us today—the question of equality of opportunity—is still unresolved.

2. *Equal Opportunity Movement*. It is around equality of opportunity, a recently discovered "good," that the equality controversy still swirls, and this lay at the heart of Boulder's conflict over the sexual preference ordinance. This good has recently been elevated to a place among those things in which citizens can expect government protection. Generally we can reduce equality of opportunity to equal treatment in education, employment, and housing. Since it is now generally accepted that government should eschew irrelevant discrimination in the public sector, the controversy narrows still further to the question of the government's posture vis-à-vis such discrimination in the private sector—private schools, private employment, private housing.

a. *History*. The equal opportunity movement is a movement that has been gathering steam in the past three or four decades, and before going further it is important to relate the high points of its history.

Following the Civil War and emancipation, Congress attempted to correct the disabilities under which the blacks had suffered, but the legislation passed was largely made ineffective by Supreme Court decisions. With the backlash of the Jim Crow period, the Court hit on the "separate but equal'' formula,[2] which enabled it to square the South's pattern of segregating the races with the Fourteenth Amendment's ban on denying equal protection of the laws.

The New Deal and World War II rekindled interest in the cause. Congress established a Fair Employment Practice Commission (1941) charged with seeing that businesses under contract to the federal government not discriminate in employment on account of race, creed, color, or previous condition of servitude. And immediately after the war, a commission on civil rights appointed by President Truman documented the continued pervasiveness of discriminatory action and urged extensive remedial legislation. But progress in lifting discriminatory barriers was meagre, being confined largely to Supreme Court decisions such as the one that forbade state courts to enforce private restrictive covenants that excluded blacks from owning real estate.[3]

Finally, in 1954 there occurred the first of three breakthroughs that were to bring the equal opportunity movement to its present high tide of success. This was, of course, the Supreme Court's famous decision in *Brown* v. *Board of Education of Topeka*. In this decision the Court reversed its earlier, tolerant view of segregated schools, discarded the "separate but equal" formula, and found the very fact of segregation a denial of equal treatment. It then mandated efforts to integrate, which, despite the resistance so spectacularly brought to mind by the names Little Rock and Boston, have won measurable if yet far from complete success and which are still going on.

Breakthrough number two has been the considerable civil rights legislation passed by Congress in recent years. The most comprehensive act, passed during the Johnson Administration, was the landmark Civil Rights Act of 1964. It brought antidiscrimination enforcement machinery to bear in areas of voting (Title I), the use of public accommodations (Title II), the use of public facilities (Title III), public

2. *Plessy* v. *Ferguson*, 1896.
3. *Shelly* v. *Kraemer*, 1948.

education (Title IV), federally assisted programs (Title VI), and employment (Title VII).[4] To provide enforcement mechanisms, the Act expanded the authority of the Commission on Civil Rights (Title V) and set up the Equal Employment Opportunity Commission (Title VII). In 1972 Congress amended Title VII when it passed the Equal Employment Opportunity Act, which extended coverage to include all private employers of fifteen or more persons and all state and local government. (The original legislation covered only those public and private employers having twenty-five or more employees.) In addition this act empowered the EEOC to bring suit against offending employers.

The final of the three breakthroughs took the form of presidential action. In the mid-sixties and early seventies a series of executive orders were issued that had the effect of changing the character of the equal opportunity practices of a large number of employers. These executive orders required that recipients of federal grants and contracts who were also employers commit themselves to undertake an equal employment opportunity program. And so began the so-called affirmative action schemes—plans obligating employers to hire enough members of minority groups and women to make their own work forces proportionally comparable to the available labor pools. A special category of job applicant called an "affected class" was spelled out in 1976 guidelines to include blacks, women, Hispanics, American Indians, and Asians. Thus, a business could find itself out of compliance with the executive order even though it never intentionally discriminated against any applicant for employment. The bottom-line figures became the measure of compliance, although the federal government normally did not seek sanctions against an employer who appeared to be endeavoring in good faith to meet affirmative action goals. Later executive orders imposed similar, although less strin-

---

4. Not only do the various sections of the act differ in scope but they differ in coverage. For example, Title VI prohibits only racial discrimination, while Title VII prohibits discrimination based on race, color, national origin, sex, or religion.

gent, requirements for the hiring of the elderly and the handicapped.

Although the sponsors of the 1964 Civil Rights Act expressly provided that no requirements be imposed for giving preference in employment on account of race, sex, religion, or national origin, the effect of affirmative action under the executive orders was precisely to encourage employers to think in terms of meeting "quotas." Moreover, the willingness of the courts during the seventies to regard significant underrepresentation of a particular group in an employer's work force as evidence of intentional discrimination, and therefore as a violation of Title VII, contributed to the same result. And so did the Supreme Court's 1972 ruling that Title VII is violated when an objective test is used to screen employees if the test disqualifies disproportionate numbers of women or minority persons.

Employers have sometimes complained of feeling caught between two conflicting policies—the policy that requires them to meet goals or quotas and the policy that forbids them to discriminate in favor of or against members of any group. These fears were exacerbated by the Court's 1978 decision in the *Bakke* case, in which the Court found that the University of California acted illegally when it attempted to remedy the underrepresentation of minority persons in its medical schools by setting aside 16 seats in each class for the admission of such persons and by not requiring them to compete with the other applicants or to meet the same grade point average. In the later *Weber* decision (1979), however, the Court found that such quotas were permissible in an employment context so long as they did not absolutely preclude applicants from outside the favored group.[5]

---

5. Other significant equal employment legislation of the sixties and seventies includes Title IX of Education Amendments of 1972, which prohibits sex discrimination in public educational facilities (racial discrimination in such facilities had been banned by the 1964 act). Title IX is best known for the furor it prompted concerning the funding of collegiate athletics, but its provisions go far beyond that narrow subject. Another

b. *Significant Side Effects*. The reasons behind the equal opportunity movement and the extreme forms it has taken are clear and understandable. At bottom are two convictions, one of fact and the other of value. First is the considerable evidence that prejudice, whether racist or sexist, remains very much alive and widespread among the hearts and minds of many of our citizens. Second is the intense belief in the unfairness and immorality of racism and other prejudice. But the movement has had significant side effects, which need to be recognized before we can deal adequately with the problem of gay entitlement to equal protection.

The first of these has been an expansion of government. From the time of the Civil War to the early 1950s the state had in practice been an agent of discrimination in voting and education, and blacks were the victims. What *Brown* v. *Board of Education* mainly did was to say that the state must stop putting obstacles in the way of equal opportunity. But, as the history just related reflects, the state soon became an active agent in prohibiting discrimination. This meant a considerable broadening of the scope and exercise of governmental power, under the banner of "equal protection of the law," "equal rights," and "equal opportunity." It took and continues to take four forms: (1) enlarging the context from one of education and voting to one that includes employment and residence, (2) extending prohibitions to persons in the private sector (employers, landlords), (3) extending protection to other minority or quasi-minority groups (such as Hispanics and women), and finally, (4) broadening the meaning of discrimination itself to encompass such activities as giving tests that minorities fail in

---

important law is the Age Discrimination in Employment Act, passed originally in 1968 and amended in 1978, which bans age discrimination against persons between forty and seventy (with a few exceptions). Finally, the Rehabilitation Act of 1973 forbids discrimination against the handicapped in federally assisted programs and requires "affirmative action" to accommodate their special needs.

disproportionate numbers and running schools with excessively high numbers of minorities and low numbers of whites. And so, in result of this, there has been not only a marked increase in the exercise of state power (compulsory busing, the coercing of employers, the providing of bilingual school programs, and so on), but also a marked expansion of the bureaucracies needed to implement and enforce the new restrictions and to handle the additional court case work. In short, the equal opportunity movement has resulted in an expensive diversion of resources to the instrumental activity of implementing law and adjudicating conflict.

The second unfavorable side effect, less direct, but of no less importance, is the sharpening of the sense of differences and divisions between groups of people and the accompanying damage to the sense of national community. This, which applies particularly to the case of race and ethnic minorities, represents the great irony, the great paradox of the egalitarian movement.

A third side effect, also less direct, is the lowering of performance levels and a decrease in efficiency. Faced with the alternative of a long and costly court fight, employers in the seventies were under pressure to hire and sometimes yielded to the pressure to hire less than competent minority members, resulting in equality being at odds with quality. These undesirable consequences do not of themselves invalidate the movement, but they are elements that have to be considered in the overall calculations.

c. *Evaluation of Needs of Minority Groups.* The principle involved is equal opportunity for minorities, and one would suppose that to mean *all* minorities discriminated against— not just blacks or Hispanics. One would suppose the law to read, "Discrimination on grounds of race, religion, or any other grounds unrelated to job performance is hereby prohibited." Yet such is not the case. There are dozens of minorities or quasi-minorities in the country with some history of subjection to discrimination. Classification on the most familiar principles (race, color, national origin, religion, sex) produces countless categories. And the less familiar principles of size, shape, beauty, economic background, and criminal record produce many more—for discrimination against the poor, the ugly, the fat, the deformed, the person with a history of mental illness, or the one with a felony on his record can easily be documented.

Yet a few of these groups dominate the scene, and even among them the emphasis is very uneven. First and foremost, and continually maintaining that position, are the blacks. Hispanics are a distant second. Some groups appear for a while as a subject of concern (the Jews and the Irish Catholics, for example), then seem to be able, much on their own, to successfully combat inequity. Others, absent at the beginning, make a sudden appearance later—specifically women, who were not added to the official list until 1964, presumably because neither the discrimination nor its impact had been seen by society as a whole to be of pressing magnitude. A recent list is conspicuous for whom it omits. Only blacks, women, those of Spanish surname, American Indians, and Asians appear on it. Polish-Americans, Italian-Americans, and so forth do not. In short, the list of those to be protected from discrimination is in itself a most discriminatory one.

Why is this so? Why the blatant self-contradiction? How can one justify such discrimination among the discriminated-against, treating some as more entitled to protection than others? The answer is an obvious one. It is the same principle invoked to explain the patent discrimination in favor of the poor in the provisions of a progressive income tax. It is, in a word, a difference in *need*.

Of the American minority groups, the blacks stand at the center of the movement because they have suffered most; they have experienced the most intense, pervasive discrimination and deep oppression, not only at the hands of fellow citizens but also at the hands of the law and government itself. Not only have they faced the most tenacious rear-guard action from the opposition in the campaign for rec-

tification, but they have had the poorest educational resources with which to resist. Under the law the blacks were
slaves until 1861 and were subjected until fairly recently to a
myriad of legal impediments to voting, holding office, serving on juries, buying property, living where they wanted,
marrying as they wanted, and enjoying the same public
accommodations as whites. In reality they were commonly
humiliated, sometimes beaten and even lynched, kept in the
most menial jobs, and pushed to the bottom of the social
pyramid in all important respects. And as a consequence of
this brutal history the blacks had beaten out of them, as it
were, that most precious of human possessions, self-respect.
Accordingly, a case can be made, where the blacks are
concerned, for conferring a special status. And so it can be
argued that it is justifiable for government to discriminate in
favor of the blacks at the present time to compensate for
government's discriminating against them in the past. Such
preferential status for the blacks can be said to rest on the
same special footing as the creation of the Israeli state after
the oppression of the Jews in Nazi Germany.

Legal and factual discrimination has also been deep and
pervasive in the case of the American Indians. Unlike other
minority groups, the Indians were here before the whites.
The latter took over the Indian hunting grounds, destroyed
their buffalo, slaughtered their women and children, broke
treaties, and finally forced them into designated reservations
(often consisting of desert or otherwise barren land). Not
only were the Indians deprived of their land and was their
economy destroyed, but they were also denied basic human
rights. They were physically segregated, their children were
sent away to special boarding schools (where their language
was not taught), and they were required to use special
restrooms in public facilities. Most were denied citizenship
until 1924, although World War I veterans and members of a
few specific tribes had been granted it earlier.

Because of this grossly unfair treatment, the federal
government did recognize that it had a special responsibility

for these people. It gradually developed a trustee relationship, guaranteeing in treaties Indian lands and water, and fishing and hunting rights. Congress has also passed legislation that singles out the Indians as a special class of people, to help compensate for past inequities.

But of what other American subgroup can this degree of discrimination be affirmed? Certainly Mexican-Americans, Hispanics, Asians, Jews, Greeks, Polish-Americans, and others have all, at times and in places, been discriminated against. But they have not experienced the same oppression or "subjection to unjust or cruel exercise of authority" as the blacks and American Indians. Neither legal nor factual discrimination has been anywhere near so deep and pervasive, nor—what is more important—have the results been anywhere near so dehumanizing. Whether for reason of a shorter history, an absence of the condition of slavery, the absence of legal barriers, or for reason of greater resources (educational level, finances, skills, or support from abroad), these groups have been able to resist more effectively and, in most cases, to overcome. Moreover, the responsibility of the white majority in the matter is less. With the exception of those Spanish-Americans who were living in the southwest at the time the area was seized from Mexico (1848), these other minority groups entered American society of their own will. The majority of today's Hispanics have immigrated voluntarily, some of them even illegally. Discriminated against? Yes. Poverty? Yes. But is oppression an accurate description of their condition? Not really.

Similarly, the term oppression does not fit the condition of womankind. One must acknowledge the inferior status of women in the United States—the differentials in wage rates, the fact that women have been looked down upon, the fact that in law they have been denied the same property rights as men, the fact that career choices and opportunities have been much more limited, and the evidence of considerable violence (both rape and battering) and the threat of violence. But they have not experienced deep oppression in the sense

blacks have. Now that women have chosen to assert themselves, they have education, finances, and skills available to
them to push their case that were not available to the blacks.
Discriminated against? Yes. Oppressed, in the sense of the
blacks' experience? Not in the same degree.

3. *The Gay Minority's Case.* Are gays entitled to antidiscrimination legislation on grounds that they deserve no less
than other minorities? Regardless of whether or not this is a
right, does common equity require that gays be extended the
same protection? The discussion so far has shown that
historically this has not been the practice; the claim to equal
treatment has been extended only charily and has not been
generalized. The reasons for not so extending it are good and
sufficient; there are, quite simply, great differences in need.
And out of this discussion have emerged guidelines for
determining need: magnitude of discrimination and magnitude of impact, in turn measured by numbers of minority
affected, resources for resisting, and possibilities of alternatives.

How do the gays of Boulder measure against these
guidelines in respect to needs? Briefly, not well. Even if one
accepts the contention that gays constitute a reasonably
large minority (their own estimate being 6,000 or 8 percent of
the city population), proven discrimination by employers
has been, according to their own statement, almost negligible. Some no doubt live in fear—fear of the discrimination
that might occur should their preference be made public. But
the data simply did not suggest that such fear was well
founded. Homosexuality between consenting adults had
been legalized by the state of Colorado in 1972. If we accept
the group's own claims about their high level of creativity,
intelligence, and education, then clearly the average homosexual has resources available to him or her (money, skills,
education) not available to the black. While the overall
impact of discrimination is hard to judge, one can hardly
allege the existence of a subjection to cruel authority.

Finally, and most importantly, homosexuals have alternatives that are simply not available to blacks and women.
As an alternative to loss of job, the homosexual can conceal
his or her life-style. Granted that homosexuality for many is
a matter of biological orientation (a strong attraction to one
of the same sex over which one has no control), but still the
individuals have a choice in their actions. They may not be
able to choose their feelings, but they can choose their
life-styles. And many homosexuals do choose some heterosexual activity at some point in their lives.

The amount of discrimination, the number of people
affected, and the alternatives available all have an important
bearing upon the merits of government intervention. But the
mayor of Boulder did not see it this way; he went on record
as saying, "I don't care about numbers; . . . I just don't think
anyone should have to live that way (in fear of discrimination)." This is a heroic statement, brave and sincere, but
hardly one well thought out. For he was saying, in effect, that
a single case of discrimination justifies writing general coercive legislation, legislation limiting others' freedom of
choice, with all the expenditure of time, effort, and nervous
energy that controversy entails. Later he declared that he
was not so concerned about rights on the employer's side
because "the rights of few, if any, employers will be
adversely affected." Here he was speaking more truly. For
numbers do count, and should be counted—on both sides,
needless to say.

*   *   *

There is a final point of conceptualization. How are we to
think about the business of preferences—preferring vanilla
to chocolate, beardlessness to beardedness, blue eyes to
brown, tall to short, black-skinned to light? Choosing may
be seen as good or bad. There are those who see it as a good,
as a matter of refined judgment, of discernment. And there
are those who see it as a bad, a matter of invidious rejection of

the lesser. Others see it in purely neutral terms. Unfortunately, one and the same word—discrimination—does service for all of these meanings. Communication and discussion can thus easily end in confusion, especially when dealing with choice among human groups.

Where the employer chooses not to hire a homosexual, one can (as the gays did) stress the element of rejection and cry "unfair," using the term discrimination in the invidious sense. But one can, as the opponents did, use the term in the honorific sense, stress the positive element, and cry "taste" and "choice." And one can further point out that, comparison being all that is at stake, rejection does not imply condemnation. Gays spoke of their choice as a preference in sexual partners, thereby implying no derogation of straights (heterosexuals), but they saw the employers' right to choose not as a matter of discrimination in tastes, but only as a rejection of homosexuals.

The burden of these observations is that even where discrimination can be shown to exist, it may signal something other than hostility to the group discriminated against. It may only be mild disapproval; the discriminator may feel comfortable with heterosexuals but not quite so with homosexuals. Or it may be fear of an adverse impact on business—that customers might not share this neutrality. The thrust of these observations is that discrimination does not necessarily imply persecution.

IV. SYNTHESIS

It is time now to call an end to analysis and to put together the results of the individual inquiries into rights, needs, the meaning of equality, and the status of the homosexual minority.

The issue at hand—and the issue that was before the city of Boulder in the winter of 1974—is the merit of *government* action prohibiting employers from "discriminating in hiring on the basis of an employee's private sexual conduct, whether his choice of partner is heterosexual, homosexual, or bisexual." The sanction behind such a proposal is not moral suasion but the threat of coercion; the employer who is charged with discrimination faces court action, in which government itself may join, and on an adverse decision faces fines plus an order to reinstate. Hence the issue at its barest is the propriety of *government's* forcing private employers into hiring against their will qualified people of a certain life-style. Phrased somewhat differently again, it is the reasonableness of government's coercively limiting the private employer's freedom to choose among job applicants on grounds of life-style.

The issue at its barest, then, is not one of human rights or oppression, as the mayor and gay leader would have it. Granted, these are objectives or ends in the minds of supporters. But even if we should assume that rights are involved, they nevertheless are not immediately involved. It is important to understand this, as failure to do so leads to confusion. For to treat this issue as one of goals only is to ignore what might be called the implementary gap—the question of whether the means contemplated will in fact lead to the end-in-view and do so at reasonable cost. To ignore this invites trouble when implementation means coercion and especially when it means governmental coercion. Exemplifying this ignoring of the implementary gap is the statement of a respected and competent attorney in town, a member of the Human Rights Commission, who is reported to have said to her colleagues, "If we believe discrimination against homosexuals is wrong, we must recommend in favor of the ordinance." But this does not follow, any more than it follows that a parent *must* spank a child who is doing wrong.

What can one say reasonably in support of such an ordinance? By way of things positive, one can say that with its passage there is a fair chance that some gays now living in fear would see that fear partly lifted, and that, discriminating employers being few in number, the costs would be negligible. But this is about all.[6]

The case one can make against the ordinance is far more potent. Not only have the substantial reasons for initiating governmental coercion not been offered, but the reasons adduced are weak. There is no question of right, little of need. What rights exist in our system, on strict definition, gays already enjoy, and a right to equal treatment in employment is not among them; if there is any question of right involved, it inures to the other side, the employer. Hard evidence of discrimination or need for protection is virtually lacking. And finally, the aggrieved have the option of "passing" or concealing their preference—an option practically unavailable to blacks or women.

So for the time and place at issue (the city of Boulder in the early seventies), reasons lay heavily on one side—the negative. Thus the sexual preference case is quite different from the abortion case, where the social issue can with reason be seen two different ways. Both cases however, end up against government intervention.

V. Conclusion: Government and Equality

What is the reasonable role of the state with respect to equal treatment? First we must ask what it is that we want and seek? Is it equal feeling or affection of person for person, regardless of sex, age, national origin, life-style, race, or color? I think not. Doubtless it would be good if strong racial hostility and associated rationalizing ideologies were to

---

6. Preference of the homosexual has certain analogies to the preference of many heterosexual people who desire to live together out of wedlock. For years this was frowned on by society and was done only behind closed doors, and disclosure of such behavior risked damage to certain careers. But in the early seventies it became generally accepted, and the risk of employment discrimination greatly decreased. Similarly homosexuality is a form of behavior that is becoming somewhat more accepted by society every year, resulting in more and more homosexuals bringing their life-style out in the open.

vanish from American breasts. But should we expect preferences, likes and dislikes, to vanish? Again, I think not. Here
we run into another consideration: tastes are a part of life
that is rightly prized, as is the variety in tastes exhibited by a
particular group. I cannot see it as necessary to the good life
that tastes—including preferences for or against Jewish
people, for or against Orientals, or for or against blacks—
disappear. Community based on race is not necessarily a
bad, nor is complete indifference to such categories necessarily a good.

Equal treatment of others, regardless of these differences,
is a more important matter, involving as it does outward
behavior rather than inner attitudes. Yet here too questions
arise. Do we want to disparage people who invite only whites
or WASPs or blacks to their homes, who hire only members
of their own social group for small jobs on their own homes,
or who join clubs for whites or women only? I think not.
Neither intense preference nor the polar attitude of complete
indifference is desirable. We want a middle of the road
approach, a common sense attitude allowing for individual
tastes and moderate preferences.

Thus complete equality as a desirable goal is, in the
general sense, out. Its achievement, were achievement
possible, would sacrifice other goods—such as individual
tastes and variety in life. But we cannot achieve this anyway.
For there is no way we could reasonably hope, by deliberate
action, to achieve a society of equal wealth, income, and
careers any more than we could hope to achieve a society of
indistinguishable resemblances—that is, a society of equal
distributions of intellect, strength, beauty.

The goal should rather be the reduction of the more blatant
inequalities. The goal, in the case of income and wealth, for
instance, should be elimination of poverty, at one end, and
reduction of excessive wealth at the other. For this constitutes a reasonable and, at the same time, a practicable goal
(one at which the graduated income tax is aimed).

The truly hard question, then, is what government should

do about prejudice that manifests itself in education, business, and housing. Even if modest prejudice is tolerable in the mind, at home, and in the club, most agree it is not acceptable in the public realm. It is not good that employers discriminate on irrelevant grounds. For besides the harm that this does to the ability of the discriminated-against to earn a living and to his or her self-esteem, it may add to problems in the community, such as excessive unemployment and poverty in certain minority groups, which lead to unrest and increased crime. It follows that efforts to persuade people against prejudice are very much in order.

It does not follow, however, that efforts to coerce are always reasonable and desirable. And here we get to the heart of the matter. To what extent if at all, and in what cases if any, is it legitimate to resort to legal measures? Here we are dealing no longer, as in the days of *Brown* v. *Board of Education,* with the demand that the state cease doing something, that is, a demand for the reduction of state authority. We are dealing rather with the opposite, an extension of state authority, hence of the threat of coercion and the likelihood of its actual use. Moreover, we are dealing with a demand for a procedure whose very nature contradicts the end government is to serve—the protection of the individual from incursions by others. In addition, legislation to end discrimination in employment on account of race, color, and sex singles out those groups for preferred status over persons in categories formed by some other principle (such as economic status, type of sexuality, appearance). And in singling out certain racial or national-origin groups as beneficiaries of protection, as the federal government is even now doing, one compounds discrimination as well as preventing it. Giving these groups preferred status over Polish-Americans, Jews, WASPs, and so on is in contravention of the principle one invokes in justification.

The quest for equality, then, when it takes the form of invoking *positive government action* to end discrimination in *private* business and housing, seems dubious to me. Except in the case of blacks and American Indians, the combination of (1) the need of the discriminated-against groups and (2) the obligation of the majority (to compensate for past oppressive behavior) is not sufficient to warrant the costs and risks entailed in positive action. These costs, let me repeat, are (1) enhanced subgroup self-consciousness, lessening the national communal sense; (2) loss of liberty—to employer, landlord, parent, and schoolchildren; (3) proliferation of state bureaucracy; and (4) the risk of conflict and backlash.

Rather than threatening to coerce employers, a more promising policy for the state in pursuing equal opportunity would be to limit state intervention in private business (except in the case of blacks and American Indians) to measures of persuasion or requiring limited affirmative action. This, I think, should be the extent of the exercise of state coercive authority in private employment. But the state should redirect its energies into more constructive channels. This entails first and foremost putting its own house in order and serving as an example: state government, public schools, and public universities should set the pace in establishing fair standards for job qualifications and in hiring proportionate numbers of minorities and women. Second, government should do everything it can to raise the level of schools in poor districts so that minority students have equal educational opportunities. And third, the government should continue special job training programs for minorities. Here is the place for government to intervene and give extra help to those who have been discriminated against in the past. Fairer employment practices can be achieved indirectly through a sort of institutional counterracism, without the disabilities that accompany minority-favoring legislation and implementary action.

In sum, we should recognize that where the quest for equality is concerned we have sometimes allowed ourselves to be carried away by our concern for social values. Surely equality of treatment—the refusal to let race, sex, and so forth affect opportunities for employment, schooling, and residence—is good. But there are other goods involved—liberty, time, energy, consistency. And to pursue equality to the extent to which we have been pursuing it is to jeopardize severely these other goods, thereby lessening the chances for true qualitative progress.

Chapter V

Government and Security: Vietnam

A third type of political issue upon which we citizens are often asked to render judgment is the issue of security—our common security. In all Western political thought national security rates at or near the top of the legitimate objectives of political organization; the quest for it, hence, is one of the most important functions of government. Our national constitution lists the providing for national defense as the fourth end for the sake of which "we, the people . . . [formed] a more perfect Union." Few contemporary Americans would not put defense close to first among legitimate activities of their federal government.

Security or defense issues present a different face from issues involving liberty or equality. The object of government action here is no longer to encourage or prohibit some individual action such as is the case in a dispute between individuals. It is rather to mobilize the persons and resources of the homeland in the interest of pressuring another government either to do something or to restrain itself. Hence it is action on a large, aggregate scale, directed at parties physically remote. Because of this, security issues not only assume an unusual complexity, but involve matters not easily translatable into personal experience.

I. THE CASE

The Vietnam intervention is an example of such an issue. The details of what happened where, when, how, why, and with what effect are now all part of history; but the lessons of Vietnam remain extremely important because they apply to security issues in general. And the Vietnam case admirably points up some of the problems and pitfalls in intelligent reflection.

The American intervention in Vietnam, let us remind ourselves, was a massive effort, first diplomatic and economic, then military, to keep South Vietnam and its non-Communist government from being overrun by the Communist regime of North Vietnam and from being subverted from within by the Vietcong (the South Vietnamese insurgents). The military phase was initiated with President Kennedy's dispatching of 16,000 military advisers in 1963. It intensified with successive escalations over a five-year period until one-half million American soldiers were in combat in the South and extensive American air raids were being made over both the North and the South. It peaked in 1968, at which time the enemy's damaging Tet offensive led to increased opposition at home to our military involvement. This opposition ended further investment of American forces. President Nixon then gradually began bringing troops home, while continuing heavy bombing and taking some new initiatives (the Cambodia sortie of 1970 and the 1972 mining of North Vietnam harbors). It ended with the signing of a ceasefire in January, 1973, and the final withdrawal of our remaining forces in April, 1974. The following year North Vietnam succeeded in conquering the South, and in 1976 the two parts of the country were reunited under a Communist regime.

II. GENERAL ARGUMENTS

American intervention in Vietnam was an undertaking that caused great dissension in our nation. It was a long endeavor, and many times during its course the American public was called upon to evaluate and take positions on our government's action. No such moment was more crucial, however, than the spring of 1968 (after North Vietnam's Tet offensive), when there was the reexamination of our national policy that ultimately led to withdrawal. The main arguments that were made at that date, for and against continuance of American involvement, will therefore be our subjects of scrutiny here. Rather than use random or selected quotations for our discussion, I have taken the chief issues—their pros and cons—identified at that time by the Foreign Policy Association.[1]

These chief issues[2]—the justification put forth for the continuance of the American involvement and the critics' challenge thereof—may be summarized as

(1) *The Enemy:* The pro side (or the side of the administration) argued that the enemy was international Communism, while critics argued it was Vietnamese nationalism.

(2) *Our Objectives:* Seeing the war as Communist aggression, the pro side argued that our major long-term objective was the stability of Asia and the security of the United States. Our immediate objectives were (a) to safeguard South Vietnam's right to peaceful self-determination, (b) to secure the same right for other countries of Asia by discouraging other so-called "wars of liberation," and (c) to demonstrate to our free-world allies that we honor our commitments. The critics challenged that our security was not at stake and that the stated immediate objectives either were not the true ones (such as protecting South Vietnam's right to self-determination) or could not be achieved (such as discouraging other "wars of liberation").

1. This organization describes itself as a "private, non-profit, non-partisan, educational organization" with the objective of "stimulating wider interest, greater understanding, and more effective participation by American citizens in world affairs." It felt the people of our country, both individually and as a group, could cope with the complex questions of Vietnam and "reach a decision on what to do . . . and make our choices known to our policy-makers."

2. The Editors of the Foreign Policy Association, "Vietnam: Issues for Decision," *Headline Series,* No. 188 (April, 1968).

(3) *Progress:* The administration claimed we were making steady progress, while critics said we were not—resulting in the famous "credibility gap."

(4) *Costs:* The critics argued that the costs in expenditures, in lost opportunities for rebuilding our cities, in disunity, and in lost prestige were so great as to offset any conceivable gains. The administration disagreed.

III. Critique of Underlying Concepts

Now let us probe further and look at each of the above issues in depth. Reordering them, let us start with the question of objectives, of which security is paramount.

A. *Security Argument*

1. *Positions*

Security of the United States appeared as one of the main objectives to be achieved by the Vietnam intervention; three others were self-determination for South Vietnam, a durable peace for South Asia, and fidelity to commitments (and the credibility that accompanies it). Yet I think it fair to call security the most important single objective, for ultimately the others were connected to it. A Communist takeover in South Vietnam and the failure to achieve durable South Asian peace would, in the eyes of our government, amount to a weakening of our global strategic position. And the loss of credibility consequent upon failure to live up to commitments would spell the weakening of our allies' trust in us, and possibly breaks in our alliances. In other words, the three other objectives—all more or less altruistic—involved finally the self-interest of our national security.

Let us review the security argument, as put forward by the American government and its supporters, and the attacks made upon it by antiwar critics. President Johnson saw Vietnam as "vital" to our security. In his version of the argument, we were in Vietnam not to establish a "Pax Americana," but to defend our own security. "By seeing the struggle through now," he claimed, "we are greatly reducing the chances of a much larger war—perhaps a nuclear war." Analyzing the thought more deeply, Eugene Rostow saw "major conflicts and extensions of the Communist sphere achieved by force" as carrying "with them a threat to the world equilibrium and the possibility of escalation into general war." In other words, let Vietnam go Communist, and a major shift in the Asian power balance would occur, our alliances along the eastern rim would be shaken, and the peace of the world would be threatened. Dean Rusk, for his part, put the emphasis on the danger posed by a China that had proclaimed a militant doctrine of world revolution and that would be a force of a billion people armed with nuclear weapons in the next decade or two (should they persist in their militancy). Because of our strategic vantage point as both a Pacific and an Atlantic power, we had "a tremendous stake" in "an organized and reliable peace" for the free nations of Asia and in our military alliances with them, according to Rusk, and this required our standing up to Chinese militancy as long as it continued.

Critics simply denied that our security was at stake. Retired Marine Corps Commandant David M. Shoup said, "I have never seen a timetable of what would be the detriment to our national interest if we had not done anything but send a bunch of advisers" to Vietnam. The *New York Times* looked at Southeast Asia strategically as a "zone of marginal interest" to us. And, according to Edwin O. Reischauer, historian and one-time ambassador to Japan, our government's greatest mistake was seeing the stakes in Asia as the same as those in Europe. For others, like Senator Gore, our intervention, far from reducing the risk of general war, had aggravated it. "Our national interests and even our existence are tied to the future of our relations with the Soviet Union and with Communist China," he said, and the war is "causing our relations with both of these countries to

deteriorate'' and creating a danger of our being ''dragged
into the quagmire (of) a wider war.''

2. *Conceptualization*

"Security" may be defined as (a) freedom from risk, harm,
or danger, (b) freedom from fear or anxiety, and (c) safety. A
secure person is one free from danger, free from fear, that is,
a safe person. For example, a person is secure from a winter
storm, a flood, or a wild animal when in the protection of a
sturdy house on high ground, or from a bandit when within a
sentry-guarded fortress.

But for all the apparent simplicity of the concept, there are
problems in measuring it. First, there is the problem of
ascertaining the number of threats to which one can be
subjected. Risk, danger, and possible harm can come from
many quarters, such as speeding cars, madmen, and thieves.
Concomitantly, more than one attribute of self can be
attacked: life, liberty, and property may be threatened. A
second problem is the difficulty in gauging the magnitude of
these threats and the ability to deter them; it is a more
complicated matter than measuring temperature or water
level. In addition, we often must also assess the intentions of
the attacker, usually with no better tools than educated
guesses. A third and probably the most important problem is
that where fear is concerned we are dealing with subjective
states, and there is no assurance that state of mind matches
objective conditions.

Yet we do make common sense judgments about the
degree of security of those around us, judgments that prove,
moreover, to be reasonably reliable and useful in coping with
the world. Visualizing the concept of security can be helpful
in making such judgments. Let us here stress the meaning
"safety" and take as the measure of safety the relation
between protective devices and threats to the basic spheres
of life, limb, and tangible property. A secure person can then
be pictured as one whose basic spheres are protected by a
series of shields that are reasonably adequate for defense

against the predatory acts of the vicious and intemperate, such as burglars, arsonists, and rapists. (See Diagram 4, Fig. 1.) And an insecure person can be pictured as one whose shields are inadequate, whose inner spheres are penetrable by aggressive thrusts. (See Diagram 4, Fig. 2.)[3]

Diagram 4
SECURITY

Figure 1: The Secure Person

Figure 2: The Insecure Person

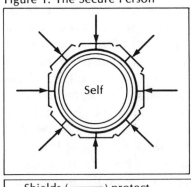

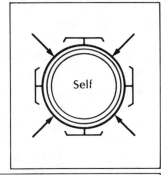

Shields (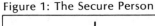) protect aggressive thrusts (——▶).

Aggressive thrusts penetrate inner spheres.

If we apply this mode of conceptualization to society as we know it, a number of rather firm conclusions can be drawn: one, over a perceptible stretch of time no one is totally secure; two, some people are clearly more secure, more truly safe from their fellow citizens than others; three, it is probably fair to say that among the more secure generally are the well-to-do, the physically strong, and those who live in environments offering natural protection; and four, government on the whole strengthens security of person against person. This final conclusion is for many, philosopher and

3. A more sophisticated view of security would look at the threat/counter-threat idea, where one has not only the shield to protect oneself but the spear with which to threaten one's opponent as a further means of self-protection.

lay person alike, the first if not overriding function of government. In John Locke's words, government serves as a "fence guarding us against pits and bogs." And this is what, to some degree, it actually does. To be sure, sometimes it does it poorly, as in our American cities today. But sometimes it does it well, as in countries with low crime rates.

At the level of individual persons, security is a passive state, while liberty is an active state. In other words, I am secure to the extent that others do not wish to and are not able to invade my inner spheres; and I am free to the extent that I am not impeded by others in doing what I want and am physically able to do. Government normally is expected to act, can act, and to some degree does act as a guarantor of security, securing me from the invasions of others. In so doing it helps me to do what I want and so "liberates" me. In this context government only encroaches on the liberty of one who wants and is able to invade another's spheres. And if we, with John Locke, narrow the definition of liberty to mean doing what one wants within the bounds of the law of nature (the equivalent of saying "so long only as you don't harm others"), then government's providing security is at the same time enhancing liberty; they are part of one and the same process.

Applying this concept to the analysis of international relations confronts us with the same difficulties we encountered on the individual level, only somewhat intensified. Yet one can make assertions applicable to the broader scale that are virtually as persuasive as those made about the narrower. For a secure nation is measured, on definition, by the extent other nations lack (1) the intent and (2) the ability to invade the lives and properties of its citizens, an ability that in turn is determined by the relation between the nation's forces and those of others.

The business of deciding a specific case, however, is not easy, since the nature of an objective threat is most difficult to determine. Even though a nation may have fairly accurate knowledge of the weaponry available to a potential adversary (the "capabilities" of defense analysis), it is difficult for that nation to know the state of mind or intent of the adversary.

For all this, certain statements can be made with fair confidence. Nations on the whole enjoy less security than individual persons, who are subject to and protected by the laws of their country. Breakdowns in the normal order (deterioration into the state of armed violence called war) occur more frequently with nations than with individuals. In the international arena there is no strong third-party organization to prevent or mediate conflicts between nations, the United Nations being only partially effective. With the lack of world government, the nations of the globe are in the condition individuals themselves were once supposed to be in prior to the institution of government, namely, the state of nature.

Yet, even though the average nation is more insecure than the average individual, nations too are distributed unevenly along a continuum, with few near the extremes of either perfect security or absolute insecurity, and the majority strung in between. Some nations are thus more secure than others, as in the case of individuals. And, as in the case of individuals, among the more secure are found the stronger, the wealthier, and those blessed with better natural barriers.

3. *Application and Critique*

Where, broadly speaking, stands the United States where security is concerned? It is no longer totally or even substantially secure; yet it is assuredly better off, in the short run, than most other states.

The United States (except for the Hawaiian Islands) has been relatively safe from substantial threat for most of its existence—from the end of the War of 1812 to the time Russia developed a nuclear bomb in 1951. The U.S. lies at a distance from other power centers; it is bounded on two sides by great oceans and on the others by relatively small and peaceable neighbors; and it was till recently the most powerful of all states. Since the USSR's acquisition of a nuclear capability, the U.S. can no longer be described as substantially secure; with the USSR today challenging American superiority in a number of nuclear categories, U.S. safeness is declining, and it will further decline as nuclear weapons are developed by other countries. Yet it is worth noting that the sole serious threat to the U.S. during the sixties and seventies came from a single source (the Soviet nuclear establishment) and that we retained a measure of protection against that threat in the form of retaliatory capability. And it is also worth noting that comparatively speaking, we were a good deal safer than many other nations. The Soviet Union, for instance, had to face not only the American nuclear threat but a Chinese threat as well.[4]

As for our security vis-à-vis the aggression of North Vietnam against South Vietnam, on this analysis it is hard to see (even on the most charitable of terms) how anyone could seriously have alleged that American security was at stake. North Vietnam's conquest of the South would have added nothing to the nuclear threat. It would have brought Communist armed forces in Asia no nearer our shores, but rather left them virtually where they were—about as far away from our shores as they could have been. It would have left the American navy still free to patrol the East Asian coast. And so one is led to reject President Johnson's claim of a "vital" interest as without substance. And the same goes for his view that intervention reduced the chances of a bigger war. For if security was involved, it was involved in the opposite way from what the government claimed. The chances of a bigger war were in fact increased by staying in, as our Korean venture should have reminded us. Accordingly, those who claimed that our intervention posed the greater damage to security were far closer to the mark.

---

4. The reader should not be misled by the above comparative analysis of U.S. security. Clearly the growing nuclear arms race poses a tremendous long-term threat from many countries—a threat which, if it persists, could lead to almost total destruction.

Yet supporters of intervention would contend *en riposte* something like this: "You would, of course, be right if we were dealing with North Vietnam alone. But such is not the case. The true opponent is international Communism." And before leaving the argument we must take account of this basic difference of conceptualization.

B. *The Enemy*

1. *Positions*

The issue we now have to confront is one of identity. Who was the enemy? Was it international Communism; that is, was it Soviet Russia or the USSR and China working together, with North Vietnam and the pro-Communist National Liberation Front (NLF—the name given the insurgent organization of South Vietnam) simply acting as puppets? Or was it North Vietnam, aided but not controlled by the Communist giants, with the NLF and the Vietcong being simple agents? Put another way, where or at what level did the initiative come from? Did it come from Peking, from both Peking and Moscow, from Hanoi, or from NLF headquarters in South Vietnam?

The administration and supporters of the war took a view equivalent or close to the first of the above. According to Eugene Rostow, what we faced in South Vietnam was "a clear aggression by a Communist regime supported by both China and the Soviet Union." According to other "experts," we were confronting a wider strategy, originating in Communist China, to subvert all of Asia. Although some disagreement lay on the point of the degree of autonomy enjoyed by Hanoi, all hands saw a coordinated movement, a subtle form of conspiracy. Assistant Secretary of State William P. Bundy put it this way: though North Vietnam acted independently of China, nevertheless the aggressive ambitions and policing of the two fed upon one another and constituted "a common and parallel threat." As for the relation of North Vietnam to the NLF, supporters of the war unanimously agreed with Dean Rusk that there was "no major distinction" between the two, Hanoi controlling both.

Opponents agreed with economist and one-time ambassador to India John Kenneth Galbraith, that "we oppose not a Soviet- or China-dominated imperialism but an indigenously motivated nationalism led by Communists." They agreed with Professor Reischauer that generally, in Asia today, "nationalism is the basic driving force and communism the technique sometimes adopted to fulfill it." To be sure, on the question of the North Vietnam-NLF relationship, they agreed with the supporters of the war that the NLF was controlled by North Vietnam through the Communist Party. But they claimed it had popular support appreciably above the 25 percent allowed by the other side. And they took at face value the nationalistic and patriotic elements of the Front's program.

On the larger question of China's involvement, the opponents were clear and unanimous. They stressed that while Ho Chi Minh (President of North Vietnam) accepted wheat, weapons, and the services of 50,000 civilian workers from China, he had pointedly not asked for Chinese troops. They emphasized the historic enmity between the two nations. With Bernard Fall, longtime respected Vietnam scholar, they believed that ". . . the Vietnamese, no matter what their political color, don't trust the Chinese." And they quoted a blast that Ho Chi Minh leveled against a 1946 proposal that his insurgents seek Chinese help against the French: "You fools! . . . Don't you remember our history? The last time the Chinese came they stayed 1,000 years!" In sum, the war for those who opposed it was not a proxy confrontation between South Vietnam and China, but was purely local in character.

A related question that had considerable bearing on the overall positions was whether Vietnam was two nations or one. Was South Vietnam a separate and distinct country or was Vietnam one nation, which North Vietnam was attempting to reunite? The answer one gave to this question determined whether one thought that international aggression was taking place and the self-determination of South Vietnam was at stake, as our government contended, or that a civil war was taking place, as many critics believed.[5]

2. *Critique*

How shall we resolve this issue of identity, one so crucial to determining the seriousness of the threat we confronted in Southeast Asia and to justifying our intervention? Was the NLF a "self" distinct from North Vietnam; was the latter a "self" distinct from and not a mere appendage to China and the Communist movement as a whole? On the first of these questions, the weight of evidence fell on the side of supporters of intervention—that the NLF was an agent of Hanoi. Though the Vietcong did have indigenous roots, control rather clearly lay in Hanoi, through the mediating channel of the formal Communist Party structure. This the State Department documented fairly well in its White Paper of 1970, as even some opponents of the war agreed. Hence our government had some grounds for claiming interstate (though not international) aggression.

But on the second question, it was otherwise. The weight of the evidence pointed to North Vietnam's independence of Communist China. Part of this evidence came from the testimony of historian-scholars like Bernard Fall. But even more important, the United States government itself obliquely conceded it. Said Assistant Secretary of State William Bundy, "We have always known that Hanoi needed and wanted only Chinese aid to this end (of unification of Vietnam under Communist control) and wished to be its own

5. We have here a problem of different beginning premises, one quite similar to the problem of the status of the fetus in the abortion controversy. One is tempted to hypothesize that many hard issues turn on matters of conceptualization reminiscent of the ancient dispute between unitarians and trinitarians—whether God is one or three or possibly both.

master. . . . North Vietnam would resist any Communist Chinese trespassing on areas it controlled."[6]

In spite of the administration's recognition that Hanoi was no puppet of Peking, it alleged that the two constituted "a common and parallel threat," the "aggressive ambitions" of the two countries "feeding on each other." But parallel action by two opponents mistrustful of one another does not constitute the danger that the integrated action of an integrated empire does. Our government was indulging in a kind of waffling or what logicians call "equivocation." "Common and parallel threat" implies greatly increased danger, which in this case was false or at least highly exaggerated, given the acknowledged historic enmity between the two countries. The same sort of looseness of thought prevailed in U.S. responses to the Sino-Soviet realignment. Although in the late sixties our government acknowledged the deterioration of the Sino-Soviet relationship, the build-up of military forces along their common frontier, and the increase of incidents, it continued to refer to "Communism" as the enemy and to suggest that there remained an element of unity between Russia and China.

Associated with the foregoing was the question of the character of the opposition, that is, whether it was "Communist" or "nationalist." The answer to this determined one's view of the threat to Asian peace, to other countries, and to U.S. security. If the leading motive was Communist, then, by proceeding deductively from an assumed generalization about the aggressiveness of Communist states, it was possible to ascribe to Hanoi aggressive intentions that would not be satisfied with conquest of South Vietnam. If the leading motive was nationalist, on the other hand, not only could one conclude that the war would not be a threat to other countries, but one had to face the implication that the U.S. was indeed waging war against a nationalist movement, whose government had a considerably better claim to indi-

---

6. Events subsequent to the Vietnam War—notably the Chinese invasion of Vietnam in 1979—have clearly demonstrated Hanoi's independence of China.

genousness, viability, and support than the South's.

In my view the matter was not that difficult. The Vietcong and North Vietnam most assuredly could be called Communist, for their leaders and leading elements were Communist. But nationalist they were nonetheless. For not only was President Ho Chi Minh, by common consent, resolved to keep his nation free of foreign and especially Chinese control, but his program appealed strongly to the ideas of liberation, independence, unification, neutrality, and anticolonialism. The objectives matched those of other nationalist and anticolonialist movements that have been so characteristic of the world scene in the recent past in both the Communist and non-Communist spheres. And no doubt the fact that the threat to life and limb came primarily from American soldiers, American weapons, and American airplanes intensified the anticolonial determination.

But of the two designations—Communist or nationalist—was one more appropriate? I think that nationalist was the more apt. One could show that the behavior of the Vietcong and North Vietnam was quite ordinary when explained in terms of normal human self-assertiveness. And to try to explain it by reference to something deeper and less demonstrable, namely, international Communism, was to substitute the complex for the simple. Given the history of the long-term Sino-Soviet rift, it meant substituting the unlikely for the likely.

In sum, it seems clear that the war was first and foremost a nationalist movement, albeit one carried out by a Communist government. The enemy—North Vietnam—used the Communist Party to control the NLF and received aid from other Communist nations, but it always retained its independence from China and Russia.

C. *Progress of the War*

On the question of the war's progress, there was considerable controversy. The administration saw steady improvement in the American and South Vietnamese position, deterioration in that of North Vietnam and the Vietcong. It backed up its claim of progress by citing favorable strength ratios, favorable kill ratios, favorable battle results, and increasing rates of enemy desertion. And it presented the celebrated Tet offensive as a great victory for our side: not only did the enemy fail in its objectives to knock out U.S. military bases, to capture a single major city, and to cause an uprising of the population against Saigon, but it lost 50,000 men and suffered a great loss of morale.

Critics, while conceding the essential correctness of most particulars, retorted by pointing out that the enemy's Vietnamese remained far better fighters qualitatively than "ours"; that General Giap of North Vietnam was continuing to call the tunes, reducing our side to a policy of simple reaction; and that even if the Tet offensive did fall short of its goals, it still demonstrated that the enemy was able to reach into the American Embassy in Saigon, inflict tremendous harm on allied forces, and sow chaos. Moreover, on the extremely important South Vietnamese domestic front, where ultimately the issue would be decided—that is, the winning of the hearts and minds of the South Vietnamese and the building of a strong nation supported by most of the people—progress had been slight on even the most optimistic assessments.

Furthermore, even if one accepted at face value the bulk of the statistics adduced by our government to document claims of progress (forgetting what hindsight showed to be inflated body-counts, tendentious reporting of government statistics, and the like), there was a basic incongruity about the post-Tet data. For example, our government made pre-Tet claims that the enemy was virtually finished; but the enemy was able in 1968 to launch extensive assaults into Saigon and other major cities. Our government claimed that the Tet offensive was a great defeat and failure for the enemy; but hard upon this, the administration requested 200,000 more troops. These incongruities were underscored by past reports of progress that had proved disappointing (Secretary McNamara's prediction of troops home by Christmas 1965 being the most spectacular), reports which, in Senator Mansfield's words, "are strewn like burned-out tanks all along the road which has led [us] even more deeply into Vietnam." These incongruities were highlighted by occasional grudging concessions on the part of individual government officials that the war was not going too well.

In sum, the government's broad claim of substantial progress could not be squared with the facts. What actually happened, and what the government generally agreed to be the facts of the case, just didn't jibe with the "victory" and "progress" that the administration was claiming. Conversely, taken in a common sense sort of way, the facts pointed preponderantly in the other direction. A rational reading of the facts told us that the enemy had tremendous resiliency and determination and that we were not succeeding in our objectives.

D. *Costs*

1. *Positions.*

As to costs, the main facts here are not in dispute. At home the war cost us in the neighborhood of $25 billion a year, had taken 40,000 American lives by the spring of 1968, brought cut-backs in President Johnson's Great Society programs, and brought inflation and severe dissent. Abroad it diverted our attention from West Europe, aggravated our relations with the Soviets and the Chinese, led to cuts in foreign aid to underdeveloped countries, and weakened our reputation for decency and responsibility with a number of allies and friendly neutrals. And finally, it cost the country we were defending much destruction of life and property, much misery at our hands.

Differences of opinion centered on the magnitude of these costs and whether or not there were compensating benefits. The administration and its supporters pointed out that $25 billion was only 4 percent of the gross national product, that the U.S. was rich enough to pursue both the war against aggression abroad and the war against poverty, urban decay, and social injustice at home, that the administration was in fact continuing to pursue this other war, that inflation was not as bad as it had been during the Korean War, and that, in any event, the war brought jobs and was accompanied by prosperity. In respect to impact on foreign relations, the administration pointed to solid accomplishments (in the form of the Kennedy round of tariff negotiations), and while conceding some adverse effect on Soviet-American relations, it contended that this had not prevented real progress in negotiating important treaties (on commerical air facilities, consular exchange, banning of weapons in outer space, and the curbing of the proliferation of nuclear weapons).

Finally, while acknowledging the loss of civilian life and the physical destruction brought about by American bombing, the administration pointed out that these were among the regrettable by-products of modern warfare, and that in its policy of eschewing mass bombing of North Vietnam it was exercising great restraint. The administration also pointed out that it showed mercy in evacuating thousands of Southern peasants from war zones, helping them to resettle in safe new hamlets and refugee centers. And it said that those who criticized its harsh measures evinced a double standard in ignoring the savage murders, kidnappings, and other acts of terror inflicted by the Vietcong on innocent civilians.

The critics of the war supplemented the agreed-on costs, but generally they drew different conclusions, largely by drawing different comparisons. Twenty-five billion dollars might represent only 4 percent of gross national product, but it also represented the scope of the federal deficit and the gap in the balance of payments. Four weeks' expenditures in Vietnam in 1968 exceeded the total cuts made by Congress that year in foreign aid, antipoverty, Appalachia, and other Great Society programs. Also, inflation was a serious matter, taking its toll in the purchasing power of every American. Some believed, along with Walter Lippmann, that "a nation, and especially a democratic nation, is not capable of having two great goals at once—fighting a war in Vietnam and rebuilding the American society at home."

2. *Critique*

Where costs were concerned, the administration had a case. The price tag on the war, especially when related to gross national product, was not prima facie itself excessive.[7] Nor were the American fatalities excessive, which at 40,000 for the period up to the spring of 1968 fell short of a year's automobile fatalities. Inflation had not at that time become uncontainable. If Great Society programs were cut back, the fault was not the administration's. Indubitably, jobs and prosperity were part of the overall balance. Relations with other nations, although strained, were nevertheless far from shattered; not only had the Vietnam War not returned Soviet-American relations to the days of the high Cold War, but some movement was being made toward what was later to be called détente (government claims on this score were perfectly correct).

To be sure, some of the administration's counters to criticism were wobbly indeed. Its retort to those who criticized the destructiveness of U.S. policy was that we were in fact exercising considerable restraint—a statement that though true was irrelevant, amounting to saying "We might have been ever so much worse." Its retort to those who criticized the loss of civilian lives, that this is an unavoidable by-product of modern warfare, was an excellent example of what logicians call *petitio principii,* or begging the question. And its retort that the critics were invoking a double standard on the use of force by failing to criticize the savage acts of terror inflicted by the Vietcong upon innocent civilians was also irrelevant.

7. The percentage of the GNP spent on the Vietnam War was only 4 percent compared to 10 percent spent on the Korean War.

But on the whole, the case as to costs was not an unreasonable one. The facts, such as they were agreed to by both sides, were not on their face of such magnitude as to dictate rejection.

IV. SYNTHESIS

Let us now leave issues of basic conceptualization and the details of the debate, and turn to the more constructive task of putting things together and weighing en bloc the two positions.

On the side of intervention, the following points seem to be beyond challenge. First, security is a legitimate goal, and our leaders were sincere in professing to pursue it. Along with the goals of a durable peace in Asia, protection of a right to self-determination, fidelity to promise, and maintenance of credibility, it was a worthy objective.[8] And there is little room for reasonable doubt that this and the other stated goals were the true ones in the minds of our leaders. Lyndon Johnson, the Rostows, and others were sincere when they talked about "vital interest," "hard-headed assessment of national interest," and the dangers of war that would follow on our pulling out.

Second, believing security to be at stake, our leaders could reasonably defend the means employed as not out of line. As we have seen above, the costs in terms of wealth and lives were not disproportionate to the objective in view. And though accounts of progress could not be substantiated by the facts, as of 1968 supporters could still with reason argue that continuance of the war for a longer period was justified.

On the opposing side, however, we have also seen that (on any sensible construction of the term) "security" was not

---

8. Later on, toward the end of the period of which we speak, less worthy goals entered our leaders' minds: the face-saving and not-being-the-first-American-president-to-lose-a-war kinds of considerations that Secretary McNamara described as constituting the bulk of the motivation in 1967.

involved, and hence, on balance, the argument fails. The United States and its people were reasonably safe at that time in respect to all alien forces save Soviet nuclear weaponry, and a North Vietnam victory in Vietnam—even if we supposed it to be what it wasn't, namely, a victory for international Communism—would not have changed this situation immediately or directly, except to a negligible degree.

But what about the indirect involvement? Might not the fall of Saigon, though not immediately, still lead ultimately to a situation threatening our security?

Proponents of the intervention believed it would. They said something like, "Yes, in and of itself, the fall of Vietnam would mean little if anything to American safety now. But it would set in motion a far-reaching chain of events that would inevitably threaten our ultimate safety." Fail to make a stand in Vietnam, and we will eventually be fighting on the shores of Waikiki[9] or the shores of California.[10] Yet commonly no substantiation was offered for this argument. And, in any case, it is hard to conceive what it might have been. For the number of conditions that must be met in order causally to join the fall of South Vietnam to a situation in which American security is clearly involved simply staggers the imagination. There would have to have been the creation of vast Communist armadas, the achievement of Sino-Soviet harmony, a Communist conquest of Japan, and the melting away of our Pacific fleet. In short, one can sustain the contention only by resolving systematically in a manner unfavorable to the United States the literally hundreds of moves in time and space that would have had to be made by both sides.

For this kind of reasoning students of logic have a name: reductio ad absurdum. One assumes as certainties events that, because of their removal in space and time from the known facts of the present, can at best be described as highly

9. Hanson Baldwin.
10. Lyndon Johnson.

conjectural. And so in the end we must conclude that
Lyndon Johnson in supposing our security to be at stake
made a point that, if not patently false, was at best terribly
weak. And those who said with the *New York Times* that we
had only a marginal interest in Southeast Asia, or with
Professor Reischauer that a North Vietnam conquest would
have scarcely weakened the U.S., or with Senator Gore that
the danger of general war and the threat to our security lay
rather with staying in than getting out, had the right of it.

The other grounds cited as justification for the Vietnam
intervention—protection of another nation's right to self-
determination, contribution to a durable Asian peace, fidelity to promise, and the reputation of credibility that goes
therewith—all turn out also to be based on faulty reasoning.
Protection of South Vietnam's right to self-determination
assumed a national "self" for the South Vietnamese, a
condition that even the Saigon government itself came
implicitly to concede did not exist. The contribution-to-a-
durable-Asian-peace argument was built on premises already shown, in other contexts, to be faulty—the premise of
an effective indigenous South Vietnam government bent on
reform, the premise of a coordinated Communist strategy of
wars of national liberation. And there was the converse of
the domino hypothesis (namely, that success in stemming
the Communist-led "war of national liberation" in Vietnam
would forestall explosions elsewhere in the underdeveloped
world). The facts of the aftermath of other Communist
defeats belied this.

The notion that our treaty promises required us to do what
we were doing was just plain false. To read the strongest of
these (the Southeast Asia Collective Defense Treaty pledge to
"act to meet the common danger" in the event of an
aggression) as a promise to wage war of the intensity and
length actually undertaken—in short, to suppose the commitment to be virtually limitless—is to substitute the specific
and extreme for the general and moderate. Conversely,
consistent with the pledge's meaning, the United States

could justly have claimed years earlier that it had fulfilled and, indeed, overfulfilled its obligations, and could have retired from the field with honor intact. As for the claim that had we pulled out we would have lost our credibility, the administration made no attempt to provide documentation or to offer proof of the anxiety of our most important allies, namely, the Western European democracies and Japan. And the empirical evidence readily available pointed at least as much in the opposite direction, suggesting that our credibility with these friends would have been enhanced rather than diminished by withdrawal.

Finally, the cost argument had further parameters than those thus far discussed. Even granted the economic cost to the U.S. was (to 1968, at least) modest in relation to national resources, there was in addition the cost to fundamental values (life and liberty). For total costs included what Nelson Rockefeller referred to as the "collateral factor," namely, the "mass destruction and the killing of civilians" that we were inflicting upon this small Asian country. This included not least the destruction and misery we were bringing to the very segment of the country we were intent on protecting.

And so, taking the argument for the Vietnam intervention as a whole, we find a lack of rational thinking. We find allegations about goals (self-determination, durable peace, fidelity, credibility, and security) that were based on questionable premises. We find the ignoring of plain meaning, lack of evidence, loose metaphor, faulty parallel, dogmatizing about evil to come, and downright contradiction. Basic to all was a misplacing of certitude and of the burden of proof: our government's insistence in treating its highly conjectural estimates of future evil (e.g., upon our withdrawal general war "would," not "might," take place) as certainties and demanding that its critics prove otherwise. In Vietnam, in other words, sound intellectual procedure was inverted. There was an almost total lack of plain wisdom, good sound practical sense, and the sense of balance and proportion that variously stand for common sense.

V. Conclusion: Government and Security

Vietnam is an uncommon case. Security has been clearly at stake, or could reasonably be said to have been at stake, in many important issues of foreign affairs. Such, for instance, was the Cuban missile crisis of 1962. Such, for instance, have been the SALT talks. And there have been other cases when the security of our allies may plausibly be said to have been at stake (for example, the Berlin crises of 1948 and 1958), or when American intervention could plausibly have contributed to the general peace (the Arab-Israeli wars of 1967 and 1973).[11]

But precisely because Vietnam is an uncommon case, we can learn much from it about evaluating those actions of our government that are directed at security. And we can deduce some lessons for the future. If one defines security as safety and follows the above analysis of the Vietnam intervention, then the following rules will help in judging the merits of any possible armed intervention.

One, *the presumption lies heavily against armed intervention,* since military intervention, no matter how benign and well-meaning, normally leads to loss of life and liberty—the very things our political heritage has taught us to prize most highly.

Two, *the case for intervention must be one of clear and present danger,* either to ourselves or to the security of others who are especially important from the standpoint of achieving lasting peace. In a nation that highly values peace and the preservation of life, liberty, and property, those who would intervene militarily in others' affairs must make a strong case—the kind of defense John F. Kennedy provided in the Cuban missile crisis. Our Lockean ideals require this.

Three, *time and space are first things, not last.* Immediate

11. I have limited the subject of this chapter to government and security, and not engaged here the other justifications given for military intervention: the highly risky one of protecting our economic interests in other parts of the world or the altruistic one of helping our friends, such as the argument given by Woodrow Wilson for our entry into World War I.

crises, such as the Russian missile placement in Cuba, are clearly more threatening to our security than some potential future crisis. And vulnerability varies with distance from one's shores, although this may lessen somewhat with the spread of nuclear weapons. Our security is threatened more by what happens in Cuba, Mexico, and Canada than by what happens in South America, and more by what happens in South America than by what happens in Africa. The farther away from our shores that aggression takes place, the less threatening it is to our security. By the same token, the nearer our forces come to the borders of our potential opponents, the more threatened their security will seem. We must never forget that however well-intentioned we are, positioning troops in Korea, Berlin, or the Persian Gulf, hard on Chinese and Soviet borders, almost certainly will seem a "vital" threat to them. Moreover, it is important to remember that we judge our own conduct by its intent while others judge it by its impact—what we see as defensive, the other side normally sees as offensive.

Four, *relative probabilities should be weighed.* Where intervention involves high costs in terms of life, liberty, and property, its justification must point not merely to the possibility that nonintervention would result in higher future costs, but also to the high probability of such costs. It is not enough to affirm dogmatically that the worst is bound to happen. What is required is to specify the chain of events leading to such an outcome and demonstrate the high probability that the sequence, once initiated, will follow as predicted.

Five, *the cumulative effect of arguments must be considered.* Even though individual points have a certain plausibility, a case may be irretrievably weak if it does not rest on a substantial base. It may be irrefutable on the face of things with respect to any single strand, but may nevertheless be utterly rejectable *in toto.*

Six, *worthy "ends" are not enough,* as the Vietnam case illustrates. However good in and of themselves the ends may be, the means may nevertheless be so bad or inadequate to the task as to make the enterprise on balance of negative value.

Seven, *the burden of proof should be placed on those favoring intervention.* In all cases in which the projected means entail substantial sacrifice of life, liberty, wealth, democratic institutions, and so forth, those favoring intervention have the job of demonstrating why we should be doing what we are doing. To suppose the opposite, that those against the project have the job of demonstrating why we should not be doing what we are doing (as was the case in Vietnam), is wrong.

And finally, the Vietnam experience has taught us that we cannot leave such crucial decisions entirely to government officials. We also need in such important matters as national security the common sense thinking of concerned citizens.

PART III.
Intelligent Reflection

Chapter VI

Method of Intelligent Reflection

The task we now face is to put together the analyses in the preceding chapters and ask what they imply about the general process of thinking about political affairs, and what significance this has for the contemporary American scene.

Method is our concern in this chapter, and method is to most people a grubby or trivial topic. Why, after all, should we waste time discussing how we reached a certain result? Truth is what we are after, and what difference does it make by what route we get to it? This attitude is reinforced by the overpowering seriousness with which methodologists ply their trade. Too often there is a tremendous gearing up of machinery for research and statistical analysis, elaboration of design plans, endless computations, and finally a single, small result lost in a maze of qualifying clauses.

Yet our subject here is political thinking, and the method used in carrying it out is a fundamental part of it. We must be able to distinguish the elements of good thinking from those of sloppy thinking or, to use the phrase I prefer, intelligent reflection from unintelligent. And so, apologetically, I proceed, drawing these elements out of the analyses of the last three chapters.

I. THE ELEMENTS DERIVED

A. *The Process*

Using the analyses of abortion, discrimination in employment, and the Vietnam intervention, we will now extract the constituent elements of the process of intelligent reflection on political issues.

The first step in the process is to specify clearly (a) the alternative activities in question (let us call this the social issue) and (b) the alternative courses of government (the political issue). See Step #1, Table II. The alternative activities we have been discussing are, of course, aborting or nonaborting, discriminating or not discriminating, and fighting the Vietcong or not fighting. The alternative courses of government, in many cases, can usefully be reduced to two: action or nonaction. Specifically, in our cases, these have been whether to prohibit abortion or leave it alone, whether to prohibit discrimination in employment on account of sexual preference or leave it alone, and whether to remain in Vietnam or get out.

It is important to recognize here that the process of intelligent reflection will ultimately call for two crucial judgments: first, a judgment on the social issue (the relative virtues and evils of the activity and its effect on society) and second, a judgment on the political issue (the relative good and bad effect on society of government intervention or nonintervention). The outcome of the analysis of the social issue will have a strong bearing on whether or not to invoke governmental action, but it will not in itself be decisive.

Step #1 is important, since it sets out the options available. A common failing is to overlook one of the alternative activities or one of the alternative courses of government—for example, to talk only of the activity of aborting or only of government staying the course in Vietnam, and to omit consideration of nonaborting or of pulling out of Vietnam. An equally common failure is to confuse the

TABLE II
THE PROCESS OF INTELLIGENT REFLECTION

Step 1	Step 2	Step 3	Step 4

Identify:
(a) alternative activities (the social) issue)
	1. Break out:
	  (a) principal classes of persons affected
	  (b) principal values at stake
	
	2. Note:
	  (a) the connections between each value and each alternative activity
	  (b) the consequences of each alternative activity
		1. Determine the impact of each activity on each value
		
		2. Compare the impact of one activity on one value with that of the alternative activity on the same value. Make a preliminary judgment
			Aggregate the individual judgments and make a final judgment; hence, resolve the social issue
			
			Then return to Step 1, part (b) to resolve the political issue

(b) alternative courses of government (the political issue)	Repeat above process	Repeat above process	Repeat above process; hence, resolve the political issue
ANALYSIS		EVALUATION AND COMPARISON	SYNTHESIS

social and political issues and to suppose, for example, that when the evils of an activity outweigh the virtues, one should straightway support government prohibition. This ignores the effects of government intervention, what we have called the implemental gap. This way of thinking, almost a universal failing, erroneously assumes that governmental coercion can only make things better, never worse.

The second step in intelligent reflection has two parts. The first part is to take the alternative activities and *break out* (a) *the principal classes of persons affected* and (b) *the principal values at stake*. (See Step #2, Table II.) It is here, in this step, that knowledge and understanding of the principles on which our country was founded are so important.

In the abortion case, the principal parties are the woman and the fetus; the principal values for the woman are liberty and welfare, and for the fetus they are life and welfare. In the discrimination case, the leading groups are the minorities and the employers; values for the minorities are job opportunities and enjoyment of equal treatment, and for the employer they are freedom of choice and the chance to succeed in business.

In the Vietnam case, the groups with which we are primarily concerned are the South Vietnamese (among whom one might want to distinguish the government from the population) and the Americans (among whom one might want to distinguish the government, the armed forces, and the mass of the population back home). For the South Vietnamese government and its people we want to break out the fundamental values of life, liberty, property, and self-determination; for the American government such values, perhaps, as prestige, credibility, fidelity to promise; for the American armed forces, life and liberty; for the American population, property (measured by taxation and resources devoted to underwriting the intervention) and, possibly, security. The important requirement in this step, again, is to focus upon each critical group and each critical value, being sure that none is ignored.

The second part of this step is to *note* (a) *the various connections,* either direct or indirect, *between each value and each alternative activity* and (b) *the consequences of each alternative activity.* (Step 2 is not only shown in Table II, but is diagrammed for the abortion activity in the flowchart below.) For example, when we connect the value liberty to the abortion act, we find that the consequence is freedom of choice for the woman. When we connect the same value to the nonabortion alternative, we find that the consequence is the woman's loss of freedom of choice. In determining consequences, one must separate out the short-range ones from the long-range, less certain ones.

The third step is (1) *to determine the impact of each alternative activity on each individual value* and (2) *to compare the impact of one activity on one value with that of the alternative activity on the same value.* One can then *make a preliminary judgment* (see both Table II and the flowchart). In the abortion example we find that the impact of the abortion activity on liberty is the assurance of liberty for the woman, and the impact of nonabortion is loss of liberty for the woman. We can then make the judgment that liberty is much better protected in abortion than in nonabortion. The impact of the abortion (or nonabortion) activity on other values is diagrammed in the flowchart.

In the sexual preference issue the detailed questions to be answered concern the relative impact of discriminating and not discriminating on each value for each class of persons—of discriminating upon the employer's liberty, the employer's prosperousness, the minority's opportunities, the minority's right to equal treatment, and so on.

In the Vietnam case we are concerned first with the impact of fighting or nonfighting on the life, liberty, and property of the Americans (both short-term and long-term) and secondly with the impact on the life, liberty, and property of the Vietnamese.

The fourth step is to *aggregate the individual judgments* made in Step 3 and to render a final judgment—hence to

FLOWCHART
STEPS 2 AND 3 IN THE PROCESS OF INTELLIGENT REFLECTION
ABORTION—THE SOCIAL ISSUE

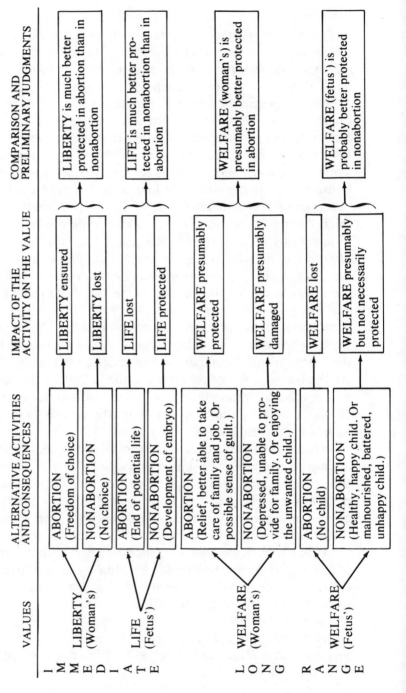

VALUES	ALTERNATIVE ACTIVITIES AND CONSEQUENCES	IMPACT OF THE ACTIVITY ON THE VALUE	COMPARISON AND PRELIMINARY JUDGMENTS
IMMEDIATE			
LIBERTY (Woman's)	ABORTION (Freedom of choice)	LIBERTY ensured	LIBERTY is much better protected in abortion than in nonabortion
	NONABORTION (No choice)	LIBERTY lost	
LIFE (Fetus')	ABORTION (End of potential life)	LIFE lost	LIFE is much better protected in nonabortion than in abortion
	NONABORTION (Development of embryo)	LIFE protected	
LONG RANGE			
WELFARE (Woman's)	ABORTION (Relief, better able to take care of family and job. Or possible sense of guilt.)	WELFARE presumably protected	WELFARE (woman's) is presumably better protected in abortion
	NONABORTION (Depressed, unable to provide for family. Or enjoying the unwanted child.)	WELFARE presumably damaged	
WELFARE (Fetus')	ABORTION (No child)	WELFARE lost	WELFARE (fetus') is probably better protected in nonabortion
	NONABORTION (Healthy, happy child. Or malnourished, battered, unhappy child.)	WELFARE presumably but not necessarily protected	

resolve the social issue. This necessitates weighing the individual values affected and comparing the importance of one against another. Here, more than at any other moment in the process, one's own value pattern comes into play. And it is here that one must give proper consideration to different time horizons and the relative likelihood of long-term consequences. For the abortion issue, the kind of question to be answered is this: given the balance of the good and bad consequences of abortion (and of nonabortion) on the woman's liberty (her freedom of choice); given the balance of good and bad consequences in the long run on her welfare (e.g., estimates of easier family life against possible future feelings of guilt); and given the balance of good and bad consequences on the fetus' life and welfare (the possibility of forestalling an unhappy life against the loss of potential life), what does it all add up to? Is the comparative impact of the activity on society on balance good or bad? The same kinds of questions can be asked for the gay rights and Vietnam issues. In this step we are required to give our attention to the full range of individual judgments, to weigh them as best we can, and, not least, to take into account the relative certainty or uncertainty of each judgment.

Once we have resolved the social issue, we must return to Step 1 and resolve the question of government action. The alternatives now compared are no longer the activity and its opposite. The alternatives now—alternatives that come into play only when the subject activity has been found to have a decidedly unfavorable net impact on society—are government intervention or nonintervention. If government is doing nothing, should it step in and prohibit the activity; if already prohibiting, should it get out? The importance of recognizing this to be an entirely separate question in the examination of the problem can hardly be exaggerated.

In the abortion example, if we assume that the abortion activity has been determined to have a bad effect on society, the political question is whether to prohibit abortion or do nothing or, more accurately, whether or not to use the coercive authority of the state against the activity. Here new considerations come into play, such as the question of whether or not the prohibition will be effective. New classes of affected persons are identified (complying and noncomplying women), and new values must be weighed. What is the effect on noncomplying women of getting an illegal abortion—which, in contrast to a legal abortion, is likely to mean greater expense, less medical competence, greater probability of damage to the woman's health, and even loss of life, in addition to a measure of deception? And what are the costs of enforcement, a question which brings into play still other groups, notably the taxpayer? Strictly speaking, what is required in the political issue is running through the process a second time using the governmental alternatives and the new principal groups and values affected.

A quick run-through of the abortion issue shows the importance of keeping separate the two issues, the social and the political. For such imaginative rehearsal makes apparent why, even if abortion is found to have a net negative impact on society, prohibiting the act might well not only not improve matters, but worsen them. For while the total impact on complying women and their fetuses might add up to a positive, for noncomplying women we are likely to end up with the worst of both worlds—not only loss of potential life for the fetus, but injury and associated trauma or even death for the woman. In addition many women would lose the right to exercise their beliefs.

The Vietnam case differs formally from the other two cases in a number of ways: (1) it raises the question of ending rather than initiating governmental action; (2) it deals with a complex series of acts extended in time rather than with a class of simple acts repeated; (3) it entails coercive action of government involving much higher stakes and bearing much more directly on the questions of life, liberty, and (for the taxpayer) property; and (4) it forces us to consider more than the direct and immediate consequences of action or inaction. Yet the structure of the process of intelligent reflection remains the same.

On the general question of government action there are two important points to be made. First, the presumption should be against it, because government intervention always entails some restriction of liberty, one of the basic values that government was formed to protect. Government action is not only costly in terms of coercion, but also in the expense required to administer the coercion. And second, before governmental intervention is seriously entertained (except where a marked invasion of fundamental rights is concerned), common sense requires two conditions to be met: (1) the impact of an activity on the society must be harmful indeed, and (2) the chances of government's controlling the activity (and doing so within a justifiable cost range) should be reasonably good. In short, there must be a serious problem, and government must stand a good chance of alleviating it.

The impact of an activity on society is not just a matter of the magnitude of hurt to individuals; it is also a matter of the number of individuals concerned. If neither of these is great (as neither seemed to be great in the sexual preference case), then government should stay out.

The ability of a government to control an activity is based partly on practical matters and partly on the existence of a supporting consensus. If a course of action is either impractical or without popular support, then again the government should not intervene. If, for instance, it is a matter of what goes on in the bedrooms of the country, where monitoring is both undesirable and impractical, government does well to stay out of the business of control and to get out in those instances where it is in (as many states have recently done in repealing laws against homosexuality). The lack of a consensus with respect to prohibition of abortion and the inability to enforce it are strong reasons for government's not reintervening in this matter. Absence of an adequate consensus and the inability to enforce the law are generally believed to have accounted for the failure of Prohibition and for the resulting lowered respect for law in general.

In sum, intelligent reflection is a process that can be

broken into four steps. The first two steps, constituting the *analysis* of the problem, are (1) naming the alternative activities and the alternative courses of government action, and (2) breaking out the principal classes of persons and values and the activities (see Table II, again). What these steps do is to break the problem into the various subproblems that must be dealt with before a satisfactory resolution to the whole can be found. The third step is one of *evaluation and comparison* of the impact of each alternative activity on individual values. The last step, constituting the *synthesis* of the problem, is the aggregating of the many individual judgments. This step puts together what was earlier broken apart, answering the main questions of social impact and of need for government action.

B. *The Appeals*

Throughout the process of intelligent reflection the question of the validity of the various judgments arises. Validity depends on a variety of appeals, different types of suppositions calling for different types of appeals. It is important to separate out the more common types of appeal.

First, there is the *appeal to self-evidence*. This involves the assumptions, definitions, and axioms of fact and value with which inquiry must start. For instance, we ask the reader to accept, for the sake of getting started, certain straightforward definitions, such as "doing what you want without interference" for "liberty." Or we ask the reader to agree on certain axioms of value: that there is an absolute value to life, that freedom of choice and equal treatment are good, and so forth. Where individual values are concerned, this appeal poses few problems. The difficulty arises when one needs to weigh one person's values against another's— one person's life, or entitlement to equal treatment, against another's liberty.

Second, there is the *appeal to experience*. Validity here is based on facts or empirical generalization. In our abortion case, this appeal is exemplified by such contentions as, "The unwanted pregnancy often ends up being a wanted baby," or "Making abortion illegal won't stop it." In our antidiscrimination case, it is exemplified by factual statements of the number of gays in Boulder or the number of cases of discrimination. In the Vietnam case, by statements of losses of life or extent of bombings. Such statements are true to the extent that observations of a multitude of individual instances bear them out. Since the reflecting person cannot in most cases make these observations directly, appeal to experience is usually dependent on the authority of some government agency, the press, or a private research agency. The validity of such an appeal is partially determined by the reputation of the authority for impartial investigation and collection of material.

Third, there is the *appeal to reason*. Validity here is a matter of agreement with the canons of logical thinking. We must make sure that our conclusions are really supported by our premises. For example, in the abortion case, we might start with premises that (1) all people have a right to life, and (2) the fetus is a person; then we could conclude that the fetus has a right to life. What is needed here is to avoid the many errors of reasoning, those fallacies that are listed in textbooks on logic. Examples are the antiabortionist's reasoning that because battered children who were unwanted at birth form a low proportion of all battered children, there is no correlation between being unwanted and being battered; the gay leader's supposition that the presence of expressions of anti-gay sentiments in a hearing is proof of discrimination in hiring; the Vietnam supporter's insistence that the Tet offensive, which was followed by a demand for 200,000 more American soldiers, added up to a great victory for our side.

Finally, it should be pointed out that there is a different kind of appeal, one that has no place in intelligent reflection. This is an appeal directly to the passions. It is usually clothed in emotive language and seeks our assent or rejection on irrational grounds. Examples are the characterizing of abortion by its opponents as "selective killing and slaughter" and by its proponents as "weeding out." Or, in connection with the sexual preference issue, the calling of one side or the other "bigots"; or, in respect to Vietnam, the use of terms like "bloodbath," or "wanton destruction." Failing to meet the test of rationality as commonly understood, this kind of appeal must be rejected in the process we are describing.

C. *Conditions*

Of the many conditions that advance intelligent reflection, three deserve special notice: *openness of communication channels, openness of mind,* and *progress in science.*

Quite apparently from the foregoing discussions, the more complete the facts and the greater the diversity of outlooks that are brought to attention, the better the mind will understand the subject of inquiry. This will depend upon the external condition of how unclogged, how free from interference, are the channels of communication. Let only one point of view be brought to the mind's attention—for example, the government's reading of the Vietnam situation—and its ability to reflect intelligently will be impaired.

Quite apparently, too, the more biased the mind is (the more predetermined toward one result or another), the less well will it carry out the reflective operation. Openness of mind is the necessary internal condition. There has been much wasteful spilling of ink on this subject. Some argue there is no possibility of objectivity in the sense here implied, of confronting controversial issues fairly and avoiding the distortions of bias. But this is not so. There are some minds that can approach even the most sensitive issues relatively free from preconceptions; and there are others that, though charged with preconceptions, can nevertheless recognize and allow for them. And where some do, more can.

A final condition is the progress of scholarship in the

human disciplines. To the extent that reliable generaliza-
tions on human behavior exist, the reflecting mind will have
data necessary to make wise decisions. Do abortions have a
long-term negative effect on the mental health of women? Is
there a relationship between the incidence of homosexuality
in a society and the health or decadence of that society? To
what extent (if at all) are Communist states aggressive?
Getting more accurate answers to general questions such as
these will help in arriving at firm conclusions on the related
issues.

Finally, the process of intelligent reflection itself is imperfect and is subject to serious objections from a number of
quarters. Before finishing with it, I will undertake to meet the
most important challenges: (1) the challenge involving the
question of sufficiency and (2) the challenge involving the
role of morals.

II. Question of Sufficiency

The process of intelligent reflection on political issues is
complex even at its simplest, and it contains no guarantee of
producing a single unequivocal resolution or perfect answer
to the issue at hand. Although the weight of considerations
frequently tends to point in one direction (as in the sexual
preference issue), sometimes the number of variables and
the uncertainties of the consequences are so great that
equally assiduous and unbiased minds come to opposite
conclusions (as in my judgment happens with the social issue
of the abortion controversy). Rarely does the weight of
considerations fall primarily on one side (as in my view it did
in the Vietnam case).

To this combination of much work with uncertain return
there have been opposite reactions. Some people, baffled by
the complexity and uncertainty of the process, seek easier

ways of reaching conclusions, shortcuts in the line of reasoning. Others broaden the range of considerations, making the process still more complicated. But each courts a special danger.

Those who seek shortcuts may speak of one particular principle of first concern such as the "national interest." They purport to cut through all the mess of conflicting considerations by telling us that all we need do is consult the rule book. The most common failing is that of too little attention, insufficient awareness. People leave out vital elements. They talk only about the woman and not about the fetus, or only about the fetus and not about the woman. They see the act of discrimination only in its immediacy for the minority member and not in its consequences for the employer. They fail to do the searching around the issue that is required for understanding. They close their minds too early. Sometimes this is the result of inadvertence; sometimes it is due to the eagerness of the thinkers to get on to action. But whatever the reason, this most common failing is characterized by under-think.

Those who urge a broader analytic scheme court the opposite danger of over-think. The process of intelligent reflection as I have described it, complicated though it is, nevertheless is a simplification. It represents a drastic reduction of the elements that enter into any real-life problem. Take, for example, Vietnam: the alternative courses available to our government included many more than two—not just "continue fighting" or "get out," but "escalate," "de-escalate," and variants within these categories based on timing, mix of instruments, and so forth. The parties affected were not merely the South Vietnamese and the Americans, but the Russian and Chinese governments, the governments of small non-Communist countries like Taiwan and Thailand, and the governments of other American allies. The values involved, as is true in most wars, included the fundamental ones on which this country was founded—life, liberty, security—plus other important ones like honesty, fidelity, and credibility. Ranges and time horizons included at least the short, intermediate, and long. Investigating all these elements and their interconnections would produce a hopeless maze of considerations.

Those who object to limiting the number of considerations are right in their premise that real-life situations are infinitely complicated, but we cannot follow them in their conclusion that every connection should be pursued to the bitter end. There are a number of reasons for this. One is, quite simply, that we can't. The mind simply cannot attend to all the variables. Second, in the search for well-grounded positions, the phenomenon of diminishing returns soon sets in; that is, as we probe outward from the immediate and direct connections to the less immediate and less direct, uncertainty enters. We can be certain that abortion terminates the potential viability of the fetus, fairly certain it relieves the anxiety of the woman. But what of the impacts at later moments? Will the woman continue not to want the originally unwanted fetus? Would the unwanted fetus have become the miserably unhappy child? One becomes less sure. Third, inclusion of too much detail, especially the less immediate and less certain connections, gives rise to the danger of improperly weighting the more immediate and direct connections. And finally, excessive reflection may simply produce bewilderment.

The dangers that beset us in our thinking upon political problems are thus dual. We can underdo. We can overdo. Yet I believe there is a middle course. And this is to hold in mind the scheme of intelligent reflection as outlined in the beginning of this chapter and treat it as a guide, not to be followed down to the last detail, but generally, as a guard against the greater pitfalls. We need constantly to remind ourselves that what makes an issue an issue is a series of contending elements that need to be weighed to the best of our abilities, imperfect though the weighing be.

III. Involvement of Morals

The foregoing account of the process of intelligent reflection has shown its inextricable dependency on all kinds of judgments. And in making political judgments a special problem arises: the question whether or not moral considerations should be involved. The point needs to be stressed because there are notable thinkers who would exclude morality as improper to calculations involving government. Such thinkers would have us confine the operation to questions of power alone—only the consequences—and would eschew questions of right and wrong. On the other hand there are those who would have us confine ourselves to questions of ethics alone, reach a decision by deduction from first principles, and eschew questions of power and consequences. Both parties normally, though not invariably, visualize decisions as falling into two well demarcated areas—one being "ethical," the other being "pragmatic" or "expediential." The difference may be described as the difference between "moralists" and "realists."

A. *The Moralists*

Let us begin with the moralists, or absolutists, who commonly see both the large and small political problems of everyday life as resoluble by consulting immutable principles of right and wrong. There is, they say, a natural law governing human affairs, much like the law governing nonhuman affairs; it is apprehendable by a faculty called "right reason" lodged in each one of us, and all a statesman or politician need do is to call on this faculty. This point of view is ancient and honorable. It is implicit in Locke's *Second Treatise*. It can be traced back to Cicero and the Stoics of ancient Greece and to the tenets of early Christianity and Judasim. The Ten Commandments may be considered to epitomize the immutable principles: thou shalt not kill, steal, covet, bear false witness, and so forth. The operation the human mind is called on to perform, in this view, is one of pure deduction from self-evident first principles.

Instances of this way of approaching decisions are legion. There was the vice-president (Richard Nixon, as it happens) who argued, on the simple ground that it was a "matter of principle," for our taking a firm stand in support of the Chinese Nationalists in the offshore islands dispute with Communist China in 1958. There was the commentator who branded as forgetting principle and yielding to expediency our entering into the Helsinki Agreements (1975), which legitimized the existing East European order; the hard fact that we had accepted this order for some twenty-odd years he dismissed as a matter of pure expediency. There was the theologian who, in reflecting on the abortion issue, ruled out as immaterial all considerations of the impact of a child's being unwanted upon its family, the pregnant woman, and the child itself.

The inadequacy of this particular formulation of intelligent reflection becomes apparent with a little thought. Principles or values cannot of themselves decide controversial issues. For what makes an issue controversial is the presence of such principles on both sides of the debate, attached to opposite courses of action. The life of the fetus is set against the liberty of the woman, fair treatment of the homosexual against the liberty of the employer. To appeal to principle gets us nowhere of itself. Weights must be assigned to values on both sides of the controversy, and they should be assigned not on an unreflective hunch, but by some consideration of the consequences of the postulated alternative courses of action—the weighing of one alternative against another. The moralist in effect denies this. Stigmatizing compromise as a matter of pure expediency or as the surrender of principle is a form of blindness, for compromise of some sort is unavoidable. The kind of predicament the moralist invites is that implied by the Latin phrase. *Fiat iustitia, pereat mundus*—"Let justice be done, though the world perish."

The commentator John Roche, who argued the morality of our participation in the Vietnam war on grounds of the rightness of resisting aggression, further argued that there were only two grounds on which one might legitimately argue the opposite point of view, that is, that the war was immoral. The first of these was that of pacifism, in which all wars are wrong, no war "just." The second was that of Communism, in which wars favoring the Communists are "just," participation on the anti-Communist side therefore being unjust. All other arguments against the war, according to Mr. Roche, were "prudential or pragmatic in nature." In other words, those who accepted the position that the intent of the U.S. government (i.e., resisting aggression) was good, but who opposed the war because the costs were too high in terms of American life, wealth, unity, and strength vis-à-vis the Soviet Union—in short, those who argued that the ends in view were good but the means too costly—were in Mr. Roche's view making a purely pragmatic and not a moral decision. This is, to say the least, very misleading.

Morals and ethics are matters of right and wrong, and Mr. Roche's mode of categorization is to say that matters of right and wrong enter the picture only in the context of ends, never means—unless the means, like war, be the subject of a categorical maxim. Yet life, liberty, and property are important values at whatever point they enter the calculation. Thus prudence requires calculation of the costs and consequences of the means for achieving the ends as well as for the ends themselves. The tendency of Mr. Roche's viewpoint is to downgrade the analytic and empirical part of the operation.

B. *The Realists*

Quite different is the realist point of view. According to

this view, politics and morals constitute two quite separate spheres of human conduct, and in political decisions questions of right and wrong have no place. Political questions are basically questions of power or self-interest, and the wise politician attends only to those concerns. The spirit is that of baseball luminary Leo Durocher's famous commentary, "Nice guys finish last," or of Machiavelli's comment to his Prince, that "he who ignores what is done in favor of what ought to be done will bring about his own ruin." Those who ignore power and self-interest are seen as idealists, as people who live in an unreal world.

"The process of government, after all, is a practical exercise and not a moral one," as George Kennan expresses the realist view. For government has the basic responsibility of protecting us from the selfish, irrational natures of others, and in this undertaking there is no room for altrusim. Moral principles have their place "in the heart of the individual" and in shaping individual conduct. But, he continues, "when the individual's behavior passes through the machinery of political organization and merges with that of millions of other individuals to find its expression in the actions of a government, it undergoes a general transmutation, and the same moral concepts are no longer relevant." Thus government cannot act according to principles that hold for individuals; particularly it may not subject itself to principles of renunciation and self-sacrifice. In this view morality does not apply as a general criterion for determining the behavior of states and above all is not a criterion for measuring and comparing the behavior of different states.

The realist point of view is articulated espécially in the context of external affairs. Among its most noted advocates, besides Kennan, are Dean Acheson and Hans Morgenthau. These three, along with many others, owe much to theologian Reinhold Niebuhr, whose book *Moral Man and Immoral Society* established the general position. Nations are not individuals, and criteria of action are "generally quite different and far more complicated'' (Acheson). These criteria ''should be hard-headed in the extreme.'' The fundamental criterion in a common formulation should be the ''national interest'' (Morgenthau); and interest is to be defined in terms of power. The kinds of criteria to be avoided are sharing, brotherly love, the Golden Rule, the principle of self-determination, the eschewal of force. Most prominent among the realists' targets are Woodrow Wilson, Wilsonian idealism, and phrases such as ''the preservation of liberty and democracy.''

The realist interpretation of correct decision-making is most unsatisfactory, because values and principles cannot be avoided. Decisions are by their very nature choices between good and bad or, more accurately, between better and worse—or more accurately yet, in many problematic cases that trouble us, between lesser and greater evil. One cannot decide rationally without referring to some general criteria of right and wrong. Some pattern of values, some scheme of principles enters into the final judgment, whether or not one recognizes this. ''Logically, there is no way away from principles.''[1]

Although the realists have a point in making the distinction between the private conduct of individuals and the conduct of nations, it does not support the further inferences drawn from it. Dean Acheson to the contrary, the acts of nations are based on the decisions of the individuals authorized to speak for those nations. The hard decisions that the president of the United States faces as head of our nation are made in a different context from those decisions he makes as a private citizen; but they remain an individual's decisions, made on the advice of other individuals. And the structure of the reasoning process remains precisely the same.

The realists' contention—that in government as distinct from private affairs we should look to national interest as a guide but not to the Golden Rule—fails to recognize the

1. Charles Frankel, ''Morality and U.S. Foreign Policy,'' *Headline Series* #224 (New York: Foreign Policy Association, 1975), p. 38.

similarity of the reasoning process for both groups. The nation's security—security of the national self—is indeed a paramount value for the statesman to consider. But so too is the security of the individual—security of the personal self. The Golden Rule does not, after all, ask for self-sacrifice; it asks only that one treat others as one would like oneself to be treated. One expects that the individual not kill, steal, invade his neighbor's home, or prevaricate, while recognizing that there are special circumstances when one of these normally forbidden acts may be justified. Is there any reason to expect less of the statesman acting for the nation? Is there any reason not to expect the individual and the nation for which he or she speaks to abjure force as a general rule, to observe the principle of *pacta sunt servanda* ("pacts must be kept"), and to exhibit qualities of honesty and respect? I think not.

It may be that as a matter of fact the average individual observes more closely the traditional rules than the average nation. But I am not convinced of it. Lying, cheating, and stealing are unfortunately not uncommon these days. And on the other side, the conduct of nations is not all bad: an investigation undertaken by the author a few years ago of the Soviet record for observing treaties showed observance the norm, violation the exception.[2] The point is that it is not quixotic to set the same general standards for the state as for the individual.

Part of the difficulty here is semantic. National interest, like individual self-interest, is an ambiguous concept. If urging it as the main criterion means uring one's Prince to look primarily after his state's security, wealth, and so forth, this is reasonable advice. If, on the other hand, urging it as the main criterion means urging a national policy that ignores the interests of other nations, always seeks immediate advantage, and resorts straightway to force in a clash of wills, then it is both unreasonable and indeed wretched

---

2. William Welch, *American Images of Soviet Foreign Policy* (Yale University Press, 1970).

advice. But the moment you get beyond this and concede that a country should also consider the interests of other nations (as in U.S. deliberations on East Europe, Soviet security, and SALT), you are admitting that another's good has some value to you, if only an instrumental one. It might be called an "enlightened self-interest." If one explains a U.S. policy decision's allowance for Soviet security interests in East Europe on grounds that it encourages similar allowance on the Soviet part for our security interests in the Caribbean, one is in effect admitting something close to the Golden Rule as a maxim of conduct. Whether they recognize it or not, realists do let values or principles intrude upon their calculations.

C. *A Proper Mixture*

It is an unfortunate habit of academics and others that they take too seriously the classifications with which they work, supposing them to be set perfectly in concrete. So with classifications of issues and types of decision-making. Dean Acheson's remark that "There are moral problems, and then there are real ones" exemplifies the habit. So of those who talk glibly of a "realist" and a "moralist" approach, of "power" politics and some contrasting term, of an "absolutist" and "relativist" ethic.

Values, the good and the bad, must be taken into account at some point in the reflective process. The only real question is how soon you invoke them and what weights you assign, especially what weights you assign your own values and those of others. Intelligent reflection, I have been arguing, involves tracing to some extent, but not too intensively, comparative impacts on valued attributes of selected groups. Moral reflection, I would now add, is intelligent reflection that bases its final judgments on the claim of more than one value, giving some standing to the values of others, as well as to one's own.

IV. The Great Traps

Intelligent reflection is never easy. It requires effort to carry out, even in limited degree, the steps of analysis and synthesis, the breaking apart and putting together that define the process, and to attend to the many variables. At each point along the way, the mind, perhaps lured by the prospect of clean-cut solutions or moved by passion or bias, is tempted to commit a misstep. The middle three chapters of this book are strewn with examples—errors of fact or of reading the historical record, errors of conceptualization or of reasoning.

There are three temptations—"traps" I shall call them—that in my experience seem to be most likely to induce mistakes. They deserve our special mention, since they can lead to faulty policy decisions, especially in international affairs. One is a type of oversimplification of reality called "simplism," the second is a type of overcomplication, and the third is an imbalance in analysis. A brief word about each of these follows.

The first trap, the simplistic trap, is the temptation to explain away discordant facts on illogical grounds. A classic example was provided by the opponents of Galileo. When they were faced with his discovery of two moons revolving about Jupiter, they denied it by arguing that, the heavens being perfect and seven being the perfect number, there were necessarily just seven planets; hence what appeared through the telescope to be planets but could not be seen by the naked eye did not exist. Similarly, we found hard-liners during the Vietnam War contending that the enemy was international Communism centered in Moscow, even when faced with such contrary evidence as Ho's criticism of the Chinese and the Sino-Soviet border warfare. They demoted the reports to the category of accidental or trivial, preserving the rationale of the theory at the expense of its validity and usefulness.

Another common trap is the temptation to offer a complicated explanation where a simple one will do. This we might
call the Rube Goldberg trap, after the cartoonist who
sketched immensely complex contraptions for the performance of the simplest acts. An example of this trap is the
tracing of the behavior of Communist countries in the area of
foreign policy to Communist ideology rather than to defense
needs or nationalist aspirations. Where Soviet foreign conduct is concerned—including even the aggressive expan-
sionism of the early twenties, the late thirties, and the late
forties, and the more recent invasion of Afghanistan—there
is little that cannot be explained by the normal self-
assertiveness, the normal fears of other great powers.[3]

And there is also the example of those who insisted on
attributing the growing American opposition to the Vietnam
war to the machinations of radicals. Those taking this
position ignored a simpler, more straightforward hypothesis:
that the American people, like any other, do not like war and
eventually tire of killing and destruction, especially when the
war repeatedly fails to accomplish the objectives by which it
is justified.

The third and last of the three great traps is an imbalance in
analysis—the temptation to treat the long-range consequences of one action as equally important as the short-range
consequences. The basic difficulty here is one of insufficient
attention to the element of certainty. For the further into the
future a result is said to follow, the less certain one can be
that it indeed will follow. For instance, it could have been
said in 1963 or 1965 with reasonable assurance that an
American withdrawal from Vietnam would lead to new
Vietcong victories over South Vietnam; but one would have
had to speak with less assurance about the subsequent
downfall of that government, a bloodbath of three million
executions after that, and, with less assurance yet, the
downfall of Laos, Cambodia, and Thailand. The impact from
a stone tossed in the water not only decreases in magnitude

---

3. For further discussion on this point, see Welch, *op. cit.*

but also becomes less predictable the farther it gets from the stone's point of entry. And so it is with the impact of political and other human actions: the possibility of counterimpacts from other sources grows the further one gets from the original action.

This trap is clearly exemplified in earlier chapters by those employing the slippery-slope argument in favor of government action: if A goes, then so next will B, and then C. If people are not prevented from "killing live fetuses," next they will be killing babies, and then the aged. If employers are not prevented from discriminating against gays, the protection now given women will go, then that given blacks. Or if the U.S. continues its air raids over North Vietnam, this will lead to the destruction of Hanoi, then to Chinese intervention, and finally to war with China.

This type of reasoning, apart from the problem of relative uncertainty, can also be criticized on the ground that in the human social world cases analogous to slippery slopes, holes in the dyke, and dominoes are relatively unusual. In the human world a movement in a given direction commonly stops short of catastrophe. People who support its initial moments say at some point, "It's gone far enough." The Smith Act (the Alien Registration Act of 1940) and other legislation aimed at curbing the Communist Party did not lead, as opponents predicted, to the suppression of the Democratic Party and hence to a one-party system. Although analogues to slippery slopes and dominoes do exist in history, cases of arrested movements are the more common.

This imbalance in approach often surfaces in the justification of government action that on its face is hard and destructive of fundamental values; it lies behind the familiar adage, "The end justifies the means." The danger of falling into this trap arises with the most controversial political issues, namely, those involving a projected coercive use of governmental authority that can be justified only by citing indirect or secondary effects.

Government coercion often leads to dangerous side effects. We have seen that what is actually achieved by undertaking a certain action often turns out to be quite different from what was intended. Harsh measures and the sacrifice of some life today may not save lives in the future, as expected. The classic example is provided by the Soviet experiment. Here the view, following classic Marxism, was that struggle, violence, and the sacrifice of lives and liberty today were the necessary means for attaining liberty, equality, and peace in the future. These were the suppositions on which Lenin and Trotsky acted in 1917, but the end they sought then is still not in sight. Meanwhile the side effects of government coercion have been appalling: millions of people have been sacrificed, lives been lost, and people incarcerated in the Gulag. The Revolution has devoured its own, including many of its original leaders. As John Dewey used to point out, such are the complexities of life, and not least of human social life, that the "end in fact" is rarely the "end in view."

V. CONCLUSION

Intelligent reflection in political affairs is a matter of identifying the major factors on both sides of the issue, comparing the relative impact of each activity on each value and each class of persons affected (for both the short and long run), aggregating the results in order to solve the social issue, and finally repeating the process in order to decide whether or not government should intervene. It is a process that embraces all types of appeal—to self-evidence, experience, and logic. It is a moral business, being impregnated with values. It is vulnerable to the pitfalls of unclarity and errors of reasoning. One who would adopt this process must steer a course between under-think, closing one's mind too soon, and over-think, confusing one's mind with a plethora of detail. And one must have an awareness and control of one's own bias.

Intelligent reflection is thus no easy matter. It requires care and sustained effort to carry out each step in the process and to avoid the pitfalls along the way. No one is going to be consistently expert in it. And it will not produce quick and final solutions to all complicated political problems. Yet, imperfect though it is, intelligent reflection is by far the best approach we have to political problems. It avoids much of the tunnel vision, emotion, and faulty reasoning found in alternate methods. It provides us with a balanced approach, an understanding of the people affected and of conflicting values on both sides of an issue. This systematic analysis— executing the steps outlined above with care and awareness of what is involved—gives us the best hope of reaching rational resolutions to political problems.

Chapter VII

Intelligent Reflection and the Citizen

We have examined three controversial issues from American political life of the 1960s and 1970s and distilled the essence of intelligent reflection on political affairs. And the question now rightly arises, "What does this all add up to?" What bearing does intelligent reflection have on our common life? What effect does its dissemination among ordinary citizens have?

The answers I am going to develop in the following pages are these: intelligent reflection as I have described it is a model in miniature of the effective use of the human mind, and it is deeply bound up with democracy, especially American democracy. Furthermore, the success of democracy depends on intelligent reflection among common citizens, and the events of the past few years strikingly point to the need for reviving this art.

I. Affinities of Intelligent Reflection

A. *Intelligent Reflection and Other Forms of Orderly Thinking*

The process of intelligent reflection stands at the heart of effective human thinking. This process—the careful identification of terms, the tracing of connections between values and contemplated action, the comparing of the effect of such action on values, the aggregating of results, and the making of a final judgment—is closely allied with if not identical to the scientific enterprise, as John Dewey so often insisted. And it is also very similar to the scholarly enterprise, where the proximate end is knowledge rather than action. In all three endeavors the inquirer is carrying out systematically, widely, and deeply an investigation—the results of which must depend partly on his or her own judgment or on the authority of others.

Intelligent reflection on political matters is an intensely moral affair. Surely the best decisions on matters involving people are those in which not only the ends are good but the means for reaching them are effective and have a minimal negative impact. Little is said here about desired ends, since over the centuries of human experience there has not been a great deal of disagreement on them. Most people, most cultures prize the same ends: life, liberty, honesty, fidelity, and property, along with self. They define "moral" by their own particular patterning of these values. The more conducive an action (or means) is toward achieving that pattern, the more moral it will become. And the more moral it is, the more intelligent it is.

B. *Intelligent Reflection and Democracy*

The effective conduct of democratic government requires intelligent reflection among a broad group of citizens, for the essence of democracy is ultimately reliance on the people's judgment. Not only does democracy require intelligence, but intelligent reflection requires the conditions that define democracy, especially limits on government in favor of free speech, press, and assembly. Mill and Milton, in their classic defenses of freedom of speech and press, were in fact making this very point when they argued that knowledge becomes clearer and better grounded to the extent it is subjected to the test of contrary opinion.

Intelligent reflection and democracy are further connected in that they both require widespread participation. There is no such thing as perfect truth, but the broader the base of observation on which judgments are made, the more intelligent reflection becomes. This is especially so since most of the ingredients that go into the process are not pure "givens" but are to some degree, as John Dewey puts it, "takens"; they are subjective elements or elements of uncertainty. Knowledge is by necessity a social affair. "Knowledge cooped up in a single head is a myth," asserts Dewey. No one person can possibly test alone all of the generally accepted facts and concepts, much less examine the relationships between even a few of them. Consequently we must rely heavily on the information and judgment of others, the value of this information depending on our assessment of the competence of the source. All of this means there is room in the forming of judgments for the observation and experience of not just a select few, but of many.

C. *Intelligent Reflection and American Democracy*

But apart from the matter of the logical connection between democracy and orderly thinking, theorists of American democracy (those who have sought to justify our form of government in general terms) historically have stressed the connection. Certainly the founding fathers did. I refer the reader back to Chapter II and the discussion of what Madison had to say in the 37th paper of *The Federalist*. There, voiced in the context of the proper way for citizens to judge the Constitution, one finds him stipulating a procedure very similar to the one derived in the center of this book. Madison asks his readers for "a more critical and thorough survey of the work of the Convention . . . examining it on all its sides, comparing it in all its parts [with the existing arrangements under the Articles of Confederation], and calculating its probable effects." He hopes they will do this in "a spirit of moderation," restraining their biases, consulting past experience, and recognizing that even the best proposals are fallible, hence "experiments," that may have to be corrected in the future. This procedure he associates with the development of the "science of politics," on which his illustrious comrades (especially John Adams) laid such store.

Most importantly, he and other founding fathers practiced what they preached. In the momentous controversy over the adoption of the Constitution, Madison and Hamilton urged its acceptance through continuous, point-by-point comparison of government under the Constitution against government under the Articles, considering its impact on such valued attributes as liberty and security. They drew on the experience of the past, were careful with their terms and definitions, demonstrated a spirit of moderation, and, at the end, cognizant of the possible flaws, made provision for future correction.

What made the work of the founding fathers particularly effective was the general philosophy on which they based their thinking, according to a thesis developed at some length by Professor Adrienne Koch of Cornell University.[1] Their greatness lay in their ability to connect action to knowledge: to harness "power" to "morals," practice to theory, means to ends, and the institutions of the Constitution to the great objectives and values of the Declaration. This philosophy she sees as an undogmatic form of empiricism or what is loosely called pragmatism; she chooses to call it "experimental humanism."

The American scheme is often referred to as an "experiment," and an experiment, as Professor Koch reminds us,

> . . . implies systematic investigation guided by an idea or hypothesis. . . . It suggests organized social inquiry in a setting which recognizes that everyone shares, in some degree, in the supreme political power. It envisages the resolution of political

1. Adrienne Koch, *Power, Morals, and the Founding Fathers* (Cornell Paperbacks, Cornell University Press, 1961).

problems in a social environment of intellectual freedom, criticism, trial and error, and a continuing process of self-correction.[2]

Hamilton in the very last paper of *The Federalist* casts his final argument for the Constitution when he asks that it be considered an experiment, which, should it prove to have flaws, will be subject to reexamination and correction. And it was to encourage this approach to politics that the founding fathers, notably Jefferson and Madison, put such emphasis on education.

Not only were free citizens to cherish political liberty and work to maintain it, they were also to be trained in the informal practice of science. In short, they were to be devoted to the experimental method of seeking truth, and this was the basis for expecting "reasonable" men, "reasonable" actions, "reasonable" compromises.[3]

The method of science, though hardly the guarantor of "perfect truth" that some have thought it to be, is nevertheless the most valuable tool of inquiry available to man. What is needed is its systematic application to "life, liberty, and the pursuit of happiness." What is needed to make democratic government fulfill its promise is a truly informed public—a public conscious of itself and of its common interest, a public aware of the consequences of common activity and of each element's distinctive share in producing it. And this in turn requires the further development of the reflective process: systematic, thorough, and continuous search for and recording of experience; hypothesizing and testing of uniformities; clear and effective communication of results; and based on this, improvement in the methods of debate, discussion, and persuasion—all carried on in a spirit of tolerance, which recognizes that no perfect answers exist.

2. *Ibid.*, p. 131.
3. *Ibid.*, p. 129.

II. ATTAINABILITY OF INTELLIGENT REFLECTION AMONG COMMON CITIZENS

At this point several questions can legitimately be raised. What is the possibility of the average citizen's reflecting intelligently on political affairs? Hence, what is the possibility of democracy's realizing what is claimed for it? Isn't it quixotic to expect the public, or any significant segment of it, to run through the calculations described in the previous chapter? And, if it is quixotic, are we not badly fooling ourselves in supposing that democracy is the best of all possible political forms?

The points are well taken. In fact, several thoughtful writers have adopted a position against the involvement of the average citizen in government. Before concluding this book, we must examine this general viewpoint. Selected here for examination are first an analysis of the contemporary scene called "the crisis of democracy," and second, some general expressions of the superiority of an elite.

A. *The Crisis of Democracy*

"The crisis of democracy" in the United States, as seen by Professor Samuel P. Huntington in a book by that name, is a disorder in government brought about by an increase of citizen participation. More specifically, he sees the crisis as the decline in the authority of government in the 1960s and early 1970s, coupled with the increase in the activity of government.[4]

The decline in the authority of government is described as the weakening of the central governing institution, the presidency, and the strengthening of "the institutions play-

4. Michel Crozier, Samuel P. Huntington, and Joji Watanuki, *The Crisis of Democracy: Report on the Governability of Democracies to the Trilateral Commission,* Chapter III (New York University Press, 1975). This work carries some weight because of the association of Huntington and the Trilateral Commission with the Carter and Reagan staffs.

ing opposition roles in the system," most notably Congress and the media, which interpret events to the public. Huntington sees this as part of a general movement against hierarchy (found also, for example, in family and universities). Other manifestations of this decline, besides the aforementioned shift in the balance between government and the "opposition," are a decline in confidence and trust in government, which is related to a growing polarization and difference in ideology, and the decay of the party system.

The expansion of government activity is marked in the first instance by the "Defense Shift" (the great increase in defense expenditures in the fifties) and in the second instance by the "Welfare Shift" (the major increases in government spending during the sixties in the areas of education, social security, welfare, health, and hospitals). These two governmental activities led to a great expansion in the national debt, followed by inflation, strikes, and other domestic problems.

Huntington feels that these problems have come about mainly as a result of a "democratic surge" and the "reassertion of democratic egalitarianism." This increase in political participation has manifested itself in an almost endless variety of ways, including marches, protests, the emergence of public interest lobby groups (like Common Cause), and the increased demands for equal rights and equal opportunities for minorities and women. The underlying causes are a mixture of long-term social, economic, and cultural trends and the general problems confronting the country in the 1960s and 1970s ("perceived failures" of government in Vietnam, in the construction of the Great Society, in controlling inflation, and so forth). Though Vietnam was one of these problems, it is not seen by Huntington as particularly significant.

The consequences of the imbalance between government activity and government authority have been a tendency of the president to seek out cosmetic successes in the field of foreign policy, a trend toward economic nationalism, and a diminution of the government's leadership ability. The cure, according to Huntington, is to restore the balance between government authority and government activity.

This is a provocative thesis. The data documenting increases in governmental activity in the defense and welfare areas, on the one hand, and in the loss of confidence and trust in government, on the other hand, are well marshalled and to the point. That an imbalance of the kind described portends a diminished role in world councils is hard to question. And the call for moderation to those putting new demands on the government is well made, and one to which this writer heartily subscribes.

However, the assessments and attribution of causes are quite another matter. To trace the whole development of the "crisis" to the surge of democratic and egalitarian sentiment of the 1960s, fanned by the media and the intelligentsia, and to pass lightly over the specific issues on which the country was so badly split at the time (especially the Vietnam experience) is astonishing. And to say virtually nothing about the government's own conduct or the quality of its leadership, when discussing the causes of the weakening of the presidency, is equally surprising. It is like staging *Hamlet* without the title role, or describing the American Revolution without King George.

When we consider first things, a completely different picture emerges. Let us take the actions of the presidency with respect to the Vietnam War and their relation to the public's loss of trust. Our involvement in the war entailed considerable destruction of the basic values of life, liberty, and property; it was justified by arguments that, weak to begin with, on subsequent evidence proved even weaker; and the judgments and predictions of the government turned out to be wrong over and over again. The presidency escalated the war in the mid-sixties up to the spring of 1968. It then leveled off the commitment and, under the banner of Vietnamization, began withdrawing American troops; yet it maintained a high level of bombing and at times expanded our role (Cambodia, the mining of Haiphong). Only in 1973 did significant deescalation begin. In the meantime government acts of deception and evasion were taking place and gradually being revealed to the public (especially through the Pentagon Papers), followed by law-breaking, and finally by obstruction of justice. At the same time the war was causing inflation and the paring down of Great Society programs.

We find that the shifts in public confidence and trust followed quite closely the executive's position toward the war and its misuse of domestic power. Is it not likely that the mass protests, the burning of the files in draft offices, and the disruption of universities, along with the loss of public trust they represented, were consequences of the war rather than moments in some long-term democratic surge? Is it not likely that the surge of democracy came in response to the perceived inability of the presidency to cope with Vietnam and the social problems of the period, rather than increased democratic activity being the cause of the weakening of the presidency?

The omission of the role of the presidency from Huntington's account is astonishing, for it implies that this key institution of government was taking little initiative during the crucial sixties and early seventies; it suggests that Johnson and Nixon were simply reacting to the onslaught of the national media. Yet the record is clear: Vietnam was wholly an initiative of the presidency and the foreign policy elite.

The most significant implication of this removal of the presidency and its initiatives from their central place in the account is that it overlooks a sequence of events that adds up to a quite considerable vindication of democracy. For the turning of public opinion against the war and the withdrawal brought about thereby is such a vindication, as the next section attests.

B. *Elitism and Vietnam*

Having examined the "crisis of democracy," we now turn our attention to "elitism," a viewpoint that questions the ability of the average citizen to reflect intelligently on political matters. This view, which sees the affairs of government (and especially foreign policy) best left to a superior few, was dealt a significant defeat by our Vietnam involvement. For getting into Vietnam—an endeavor accepted as a mistake in retrospect, both generally and by many of its architects—was the work of a few, while getting out was the work of the many.

Responsibility for our deep entanglement in Vietnam falls disproportionately upon a small circle of national leaders. Particularly, it falls upon a small group in the executive branch—upon the brothers Bundy, Rostow, and Dulles, and the Deans Acheson and Rusk, not to mention, of course, the Chief Executives themselves and their secretaries of defense and military advisers. For these gentlemen, after all, made the key decisions; they made them commonly without consulting the Congress; they considered the public only from the point of view of the limits of its tolerance. This small group, moreover, formed an elite in the very best sense of the term. They were men of extraordinary ability and dedication: men of consummate political skill, like Lyndon Johnson; men of great integrity, like Dean Acheson and Dwight Eisenhower; men of exemplary patience and decency, like Dean Rusk, men of unflagging energy and industry, like Robert McNamara; and men of brilliance of mind, like McGeorge Bundy. Although considerations of pride and power cannot be entirely ruled out as factors in the wrong decisions they made (*vide* the Pentagon Papers), they did not make these decisions out of petty motives or stupidity.

Only when it became apparent that their policies were pressing against the limit of what the public would tolerate did this small group of elite reluctantly change its policies and reverse direction. Lyndon Johnson dramatically called off the bombing of North Vietnam in April, 1968, and announced his decision not to run for reelection—but only after Dean Acheson, on behalf of a committee of advisors from outside the government, had informed him he no longer had the country behind him. Melvin Laird put his support of deescalation and withdrawal from Vietnam not in terms of personal conviction (for that, he said, argued the opposite course) but in terms of the need to conform to the wishes of the people. Richard Nixon has at times strongly suggested he harbored similar sentiments.

It is true that up to 1968 the major decisions made by these men received majority support from the public. But much of this support was based on the government's presentation of its case, which was anything but straightforward. Public support was reluctant and hesitant, tendered out of deference to the president's supposedly greater access to the facts and to his superior wisdom. The president has considerable power to create opinion, and there are reasons for believing that had Presidents Kennedy and Johnson taken a softer tack, they would have secured an even larger and firmer majority, for the war was widely acknowledged to be unpopular, even by leading supporters. Subsequent moves toward peace received resounding approval. One cannot help being impressed in this connection by the extraordinarily high percentages of public support given accommodating moves such as Richard Nixon's signing of the SALT pacts and rapproachement with Moscow and Peking, by the large contribution these made to his landslide reelection, and by the rise in his popularity occasioned by the final bringing off of the cease-fire.

While the public supported the government in the beginning, it did so reluctantly, on the misleading and tendentious interpretation of what was going on. It was the first to turn against the war, virtually compelling the government to follow. The public refused to let the government's faulty perspectives on a war against Communism override its own sense of proportion. And in all this it did well.

The change in opinion, the antiwar sentiment rising from about 24 percent in August, 1965, to 61 percent six years later, was concentrated largely in the first few months of 1968, when it took a quantum leap.[5] To reiterate (from Chapter V), this leap occurred shortly after the celebrated Tet offensive. Although not entirely successful from North Vietnam's point of view, the offensive resulted in a smashing invasion of Saigon and other major cities in the South, causing much death and destruction. Moreover, the assault was carried out by an enemy that for several years had constantly been presented by our government as worn out. And it was followed almost immediately by a request for 200,000 more American troops, an augmentation by one-third of our forces then in the field. In short, what actually happened just did not tally with the victory our government represented it to be. The public was no longer buying the involved and sophisticated interpretations offered by our government. The public was giving preference at last to its own plain reading of what was going on, tied closely to the evidence of its senses.

And the public did well and rightly in this, playing out loyally and intelligently the role assigned it in our political order. For long years it had stuck steadfastly, if reluctantly, with the government and its leaders, giving them the benefit of the doubt in a series of cases of ever-increasing misjudgment, ever-enlarging divergence between prediction and performance. The public supported the government loyally

5. According to a study done at the University of Michigan, the American public, two-to-one hawkish in January, 1968, had by April become on balance dovish and by the end of the year, two-to-one dovish. Reasons most often given were of a more practical than moral turn— failure to win, high cost in American life and limb. Most interestingly, the study found the shift largely unrelated to the antiwar movement and campus protests (to which a large part of the public was hostile); the latter, having peaked earlier, appealed far more to such moral considerations as the death and destruction the U.S. was wreaking on the Vietnamese.

until the discordancies became too glaring: It would have done wrongly not to have changed. For the government had by this time, by its own actions, forfeited the right to be believed. It had, in an inversion of the old fable, cried "Lamb" once too often. It had exhausted its credit.

Elitist theory, which has enjoyed considerable vogue in recent years, would keep public participation in government at a minimum, upon the supposition that the public that participates least participates best. Articulators of this view include alike prominent defenders of and detractors from recent policy. Among the defenders there is Dean Acheson, through whose *Present at the Creation* runs the conviction that if only the public (and the press and Congress) would "stay the course" and continue backing executive policies, or at least refrain from criticizing and intervening—all would be well. There is Eugene Rostow, who imputes to public opinion "a formidable power to resist' information and advice which contradict what it wishes to believe." He sees the key problem of American foreign policy to be whether the public will be steadfast enough in backing further presidential interventions of the Korea, Greece, and Vietnam types. There is Vice-President Agnew, who, in a speech at Chicago during the 1972 campaign, said that "the complexities of the nuclear age rule out a foreign policy conducted by consensus" and then congratulated the country for the fact that the critical decisions in such matters were vested in the president rather than in Congress or other groups.

Among the detractors and critics of recent policy who share this same view is Hans Morgenthau, who affirms of the "popular mind" that, "unaware of the fine distinctions of the statesman's thinking, [it] reasons more often than not in the simple moralistic and legalistic terms of absolute good and absolute evil." And there is Walter Lippmann, who in the following passage from his *Public Philosophy* defends giving the executive wide latitude and speaks against giving the same to Congress, which he sees as representative of the public.

> The unhappy truth is that the prevailing public opinion has been destructively wrong at the critical junctures. The people have imposed a veto upon the judgment of informed and responsible officials. They have compelled the governments, which usually knew what would have been wiser or was necessary or was more expedient, to be too late with too little, or too long with too much, too pacifist in peace and too bellicose in war. . . .There is no mystery about why there is such a tendency for popular opinion to be wrong in judging war and peace. Strategic and diplomatic decisions call for a kind of knowledge—not to speak of an experience and a seasoned judgment—which cannot be had by glancing at the newspapers.

Yet where Vietnam is concerned, it is hard to see why the various failings ascribed by Lippmann and others to the average citizens are not more properly ascribed to their leaders.

C. *A Summary View*

The real question raised by democracy is not whether average citizens commonly reflect intelligently on political matters; they don't. It is not even whether they reflect as well as un-average citizens, the so-called elite. They may fall short here, though this is far from clear. It is not whether we should have elites: we have them, whether we want them or not.

The really crucial question is whether any elite—any grouping of "the best and the brightest"—can be wide enough and good enough to justify the curtailing of those features of government that define limited democracy, namely, the limitations on government found in the Constitution and the rather modest control assigned the average citizen (the right to pass judgment on general programs and persons at periodic elections, the right to initiate legislation and amendments, the right to lobby or protest, and so forth).

The experience of the past two decades underscores the strength of the democratic system. It underlines the Jeffersonian belief that the people are the only safe repository of the ultimate power of government. Partly it does so by demonstrating in the turn-around on Vietnam that the average citizen, by virtue of having knowledge of an unspecialized nature (or by virtue of wearing the shoe, being a better judge of where it pinches than the cobbler), not only may but is likely to maintain the more balanced perspective. And partly it does so by demonstrating how egregiously wrong an elite can be.

Above all, the experience of the last two decades underlines the fact that the common citizen has as much potential for reflecting intelligently as the elite. Vietnam showed us that the very core of this process—the recognition of valued attributes on each side of the issue and the weighing of one against another—was noticeably lacking among the elite. Those in power were too close to the war, too committed to a policy, and too one-sided in their outlook. But the rudiments of the process, the weighing and balancing of elements on both sides of the controversy, showed up among the rank and file and finally led to the proper ordering of our political thinking.

III. The Contemporary American Crisis

The preceding discussion suggests that in the coming years we face two threats instead of one: not only the one from the left (what Huntington calls the surge of democracy), but one from the right as well. To the conventional assessment of the dangers represented by the equality-mongers on one side should be added the dangers represented by the security-mongers on the other side. To the risks of too little respect for authority should be added the risk of too much respect, such as supported the foreign policy failures of the late sixties and that may be with us again if new crises arise—regarding the Mid-East situation, the breakdown of détente, nuclear proliferation, or whatever. To the risk of an excess of democracy in one area should be added the risk of a deficiency in another. We are not talking here, be it understood, of menaces from the far right and far left, such as confronted Weimar Germany. At issue is something of lesser magnitude—the possibility of "distempers" or imbalances from those on the near right and near left. Even so, the problems are not such as can be safely overlooked.

For plainly Huntington's analysis of "the crisis of democracy" is correct as far as it goes. There is abroad an excessive disrespect for authority, on whatever principle it may be based, whatever the association or institution involved (government, family, university). There is also a demand for liberty in the sense of an absence of institutional restrictions of all sorts.

The excesses of the near left group are manifold. The constant cry is for liberty and for equal rights. But when its members cry for liberty, they forget that in a normal society absolute liberty for all is impossible. When they demand respect for "rights," they forget that rights—in the strict sense of liberties protected by the Constitution—are almost without exception rights against the government. And when they cry for equality, they forget that positive governmental action in favor of an underprivileged group can be undertaken only at the expense of someone else's liberty. They forget that requiring affirmative action and fulfillment of quotas for certain minorities will end up in unfair treatment not only of some members of the majority, but also of members of other minority groups. They forget that the effort to correct one inequity unavoidably creates another, and they overlook the distinction between those who have experienced real oppression and those whose life-styles are a matter of choice.

The deficiencies of the near right are less apparent. This group contains more elements than the foreign policy establishment; for example, it contains that significant segment of representatives of corporate wealth who, for all their proclamations of devotion to laissez-faire, expect as their due (and in large measure receive) great favors from government. But the deficiencies of the foreign policy establishment are representative of the general weaknesses of the entire near right. Those deficiencies include, first, a distorted view of the Communist movement, and second (and more importantly), a mistaken theory of international affairs—together adding up to a lack of true discrimination or discretion in world views. Out of these has come a greatly inflated view of external threats to America and of the requirements of security. And from this in turn has come an approach to American foreign policy that starts at the wrong end and poses needless dangers to the system. Just because the individual personalities holding these views have been men of high calibre does not make such views truths, nor does it alter the fact that such views pose a danger to the system; indeed, it may add to that danger.

The defective image of the Communist world referred to is one which, in the face of much evidence, denies the effective disunity of the movement, denies the historical possibility of a Communist regime's acquiring significant popular support, and, accordingly, denies the compatibility of Communism and nationalism and the practicability of a Communist-led but still genuinely nationalist force. This highly questionable view of international relations, referred to as "realism," makes much of the notion of balance-of-power. It denies (even in the face of such hard evidence as the Sino-Soviet split) that power normally balances power in the Eurasian world even without American military intervention, and asserts that America has a "vital" interest in what goes on in Europe and even in other parts of the Eurasian continent. The result is an image of our security clearly and presently affected—not remotely and distantly—by what happens in France, Britain, or Japan, and, for some, what happens in Vietnam, Korea, or Afghanistan. It is to say that American security is equally threatened by what happens in these distant areas as by what happens in Canada, Mexico, or Cuba.

A further consequence of this view is to turn upside down the normal thinking process and put the presumption in favor of "hard" policies. For obviously, if the national security is truly at stake, it is up to the dissenter to show that dispatching task forces, sharing of nuclear know-how, issuing threats to other powers is not in order. Part of this turning upside down of normal thinking processes—this looking through the wrong end of the telescope—is a misplacement of certitude. Instead of placing this where it belongs, on present or near-run costs (the least speculative of the elements in the equation), it is placed on long-run results (the most speculative).

A still further consequence is the needless burden this mode of thinking puts on the domestic system. This is not merely the burden of larger defense budgets and the stimulation of inflationary pressures; it is also, and more importantly, the risk of erosion of the basic democratic safeguards. For if our own security is thought to be clearly and presently endangered, not only is the burden of justification shifted to the critic and away from the supporter of large defense expenditures, but it is shifted also to the critic of such measures as the draft, laws against divulging state secrets, engagement in "dirty tricks," and so forth. The question is no longer, "Do we really need the draft?" but becomes, rather, "Can we afford not to have one?" To this impact of its foreign policy orientation on the domestic scene, the foreign policy establishment has been singularly blind. And it has overlooked one of the great truths so clearly perceived by Madison, Hamilton, and the other founding fathers, namely, that the pursuit of defense abroad may lead to tyranny at home.

The political problem of our day, or, if you will, the real crisis of democracy, is marked by inordinate demands not simply from one end of the spectrum, but from both. The demands for greater security are matched on the other side by the demands for greater equality. Each side feeds on the other, and together they result in Big Government. The shifts in load that have resulted—first, the Defense Shift, then the Welfare Shift—have produced an unbalanced budget, contributing heavily to the problem of inflation. Each side recognizes the danger of over-government. But the remedy each characteristically finds is to cut back on demands of the other.

How does one characterize the crisis from the perspective of its bearings on democracy? On the analysis given by Huntington, to say democracy is suffering for intrinsic reasons—for having too much of that which defines it—contains at most only part of the answer. What we suffer from today, I think it more correct to say, is excessive and disproportionate quests for security as well as equality, each quest fueled and distorted by incomplete perceptions of the world round-about. And the first of the two movements constitutes the greater, though more intermittent, peril to those features that define democracy (openness, cognizance of fundamental freedoms, responsibility).

IV. CONCLUSION

Events of recent years have demonstrated many failings in our government, both in domestic areas and in foreign policy. Government has been overzealous in its efforts to provide equality and security. In so doing, it has lost sight of one of its primary purposes—that of protecting the liberty of the individual. It has become bogged down in its own bureaucracy. It is even misusing its power. When government goes awry, it needs to be reexamined. There is no better place to start (as in any area of human concern) than to return to fundamentals. And fundamentals, where American political matters are at issue, take us back to the thinking of John Locke and the founding fathers, to the theory of limited democracy.

Government in its most elemental form, as we stated in Chapter II, is a device for protecting the life, liberty, and property of the individual from the most serious invasions of fellow citizens. This is its core justification. Since the accomplishment of this objective ultimately entails the use of force (or the threat of it), government is distinguished by its monopoly of legitimate coercion.

But power, most especially the power legitimately to coerce, can be abused and, as the most cursory examination of the historical record reveals, often has been abused. This gives rise to the "dilemma of government": how to provide government with enough power to do its job, while at the same time preventing abuse of power.

The answer to this dilemma that John Locke gave was to limit drastically the scope of government and the manner in which coercive authority was to be used, to provide in the separation of powers and other institutional arrangements a system of checks and balances, and to preserve a right to revolt. Within this general scheme the founders stayed closely. While admitting some enlargement of the scope of authority to include, for instance, education, they emphasized limits, made detailed provision in the forms of reserved rights, both substantive and procedural, and, finally, provided for a form of popular government that answers in the main to what we understand democracy to mean.

The founding fathers thus gave us a "limited democracy," a government that has clear limits with respect to the scope of governmental authority and means of control and one that places ultimate responsibility in the hands of the people. It is a government characterized by moderateness—one providing for some popular participation, but not too much, and giving some power to those who govern, but not too much. It is a government premised on clear-cut values, the end in view being the modest one of security, justice, and welfare for the individual. Finally, this government is to be considered at best only an experiment and is to be changed and improved upon as needed, while keeping in mind all the time its main function.

But the founding fathers gave us more than a limited democracy. They showed us, in theory as well as in practice, how to reflect intelligently on political matters. They stressed the importance of starting with clear ideas, framing alternative courses of action, examining the subject on all sides, criticizing it, comparing parts, and calculating consequences. And they stressed the importance of moderation and of allowing for one's own biases.

The founding fathers recognized that there is no such thing as perfect truth and that decisions involving questions of government action are never easy. They recognized that government intervention in order to protect one individual's life, liberty, or property might encroach on the life, liberty, or property of another. And so with Locke they concluded that the presumption should be against government intervention; only when government action clearly improves the total impact on society should government intervene.

In the two hundred years since the establishment of our limited democracy, the scope of government has been greatly expanded from the limited one of protecting the individual's life, liberty, and property. Government has not only assumed the primary responsibility for education (a responsibility that Jefferson and several of his associates saw as an important duty of government, if democracy was to succeed), but it has embraced new and expanding roles in health, welfare, housing, transportation, and other areas of economic, social, and political concern. On the international scene, government has greatly expanded its role from the limited one envisioned by the founding fathers of protecting citizens from foreign aggression.

This growth in scope of authority has led to a complexity and unwieldiness that make it hard for government to achieve a balance in seeking its primary ends. Some of this expansion is clearly justified in a society that feels some responsibility for the welfare, equality, and justice of fellow citizens and in a world where countries have become increasingly interrelated. But much of this expansion is at best dubious and at worst downright dangerous. The critique of government today is that, on the one hand, it has been performing poorly its primary task of protecting the fundamental liberties of its citizens, while, on the other hand, it has been squandering its resources in misguided efforts to perform functions that lie at best on the periphery of its legitimate sphere of responsibility—efforts to create an international order abroad in which free societies can flourish and to establish Utopian social justice at home. It has, paraphrasing the Book of Common Prayer, left undone those things which it ought to have done, and done those things which it ought not to have done.

A strategy for correcting our ills, as it seems to me, should (1) start with a revitalization of the main tasks of government, especially the prevention and control of crime and the provision of education, (2) proceed, where other less fundamental activities are concerned, to emphasizing ways of helping all the poor rather than certain minorities (with the accent on developing simpler and more effective programs), and (3) end with maintaining a lower posture in international affairs. Above all, because it touches the fundamentals of our system, we must see to the elimination of those practices that, in the name of national security, have compromised open, responsible government. We must continue to resist the blandishments of those who believe the cure for the evils of democracy is less democracy, especially in the curtailment of openness and the fundamental rights of free speech and a free press.

Our case studies have demonstrated what the founding fathers knew—that the values of one individual may conflict with the values of another individual, that the liberty of one person may conflict with the security of another. And this leads to the question of how government may best protect the values on both sides of a controversy. One is reminded of the story of the man who was arrested for swinging his arms and hitting a passerby in the nose. The accused remonstrated in court, "Hasn't a man a right to swing his arms in a free country?" The judge replied, "Your right to swing your arms stops just where the other man's nose begins."

It is this conflict of values that is at the root of most political controversies. Too often antagonists see only the values on one side of an issue and overlook the values on the other. They fail to understand that government intervention to secure values for one set of individuals may deprive another set of individuals of equally important values. Some of the failures of our government in recent years, especially in foreign policy, are the results of the inability of our ruling elite to understand both sides of an issue. And this is the very reason the founding fathers retained the ultimate power in the hands of the people. The importance of the common citizen in monitoring the performance of the ruling elite is well illustrated in our Vietnam case study, where citizens showed a greater sensitivity than the elite to the elements on both sides of the issue.

What makes government responsive to the people is the assignment of the right to vote to all or almost all of the governed. But the exercise of this right by all in every election is not essential. Like the proverbial gun behind the door, it is sufficient that it be there. As long as government has to reckon with the possibility of the use of this right in the future, those in authority will be heedful of the interest of those they govern.

It is the quality of reflection on the part of the citizens who participate, not the number of citizens who participate at any one specific election, that is the heart of successful democracy. What is needed is the building up in ourselves of the habit of intelligent reflection. We need to reflect more intelligently upon our problems and the positions of candidates for public office. We need to redirect our energies and shift our focus from getting out the vote to where it really belongs—on the exercise of intelligent reflection.

The art of intelligent reflection on political issues requires an understanding of our political heritage—of the theory on which our government is premised and of the values that we prize. Applying this theory to our analysis of contemporary problems enables us better to understand the elements on both sides of a controversy and better to determine when and how government should intervene in the affairs of the people. If we, both as individuals and as a nation, are to cope with the many problems that lie ahead, we need to make a more conscious effort to carry out the various steps in the process of intelligent reflection. We need to do this in a spirit of tolerance, which recognizes that perfect answers to problems are out of the question, and with a renewed willingness to learn from experience. Only if we do this will we achieve what Jefferson called the "common sense" of the matter.

Appendix

Appendix

THE DECLARATION OF INDEPENDENCE
July 4, 1776

The second Continental Congress (May 10, 1755) was assembled to unite the colonists in their struggle against English rule. Armed conflict at Lexington and Concord the previous month had marked the beginning of revolutionary warfare.

Acting as a central government for all the colonies, the Congress organized a Federal army and named Washington its commander. It also set up machinery for financing the war, regulating trade, and conducting diplomatic relations with other countries.

On July 4, 1776 Jefferson's draft of the Declaration of Independence was adopted. It was a powerful instrument in rallying the colonists at home and in winning aid from freedom-loving forces abroad.

*W*hen, in the course of human events, it becomes necessary for one people to dissolve the political bands which have connected them with another, and to assume, among the powers of the earth, the separate and equal station to which the laws of nature and of nature's God entitle them, a decent respect to the opinions of mankind requires that they should declare the causes which impel them to the separation.

We hold these truths to be self-evident, that all men are created equal; that they are endowed by their Creator with certain unalienable rights; that among these, are life, liberty, and the pursuit of happiness. That, to secure these rights, governments are instituted among men, deriving their just powers from the consent of the governed; that, whenever any form of government becomes destructive of these ends, it is the right of the people to alter or to abolish it, and to institute a new government, laying its foundation on such principles, and organizing its powers in such form, as to them shall seem most likely to effect their safety and happiness. Prudence, indeed, will dictate that governments long established, should not be changed for light and transient causes; and, accordingly, all experience hath shown, that mankind are more disposed to suffer, while evils are sufferable, than to right themselves by abolishing the forms to which they are accustomed. But, when a long train of abuses and usurpations, pursuing invariably the same object, evinces a design to reduce them under absolute despotism, it is their right, it is their duty, to throw off such government and to provide new guards for their future security. Such has been the patient sufferance of these colonies, and such is now the necessity which constrains them to alter their former systems of government. The history of the present King of Great Britain is a history of repeated injuries and usurpations, all having, in direct object, the establishment of an absolute tyranny over these States. To prove this, let facts be submitted to a candid world:—

He has refused his assent to laws the most wholesome and necessary for the public good.

He has forbidden his governors to pass laws of immediate and pressing importance, unless suspended in their operation till his assent should be obtained; and, when so suspended, he has utterly neglected to attend to them.

He has refused to pass other laws for the accommodation of large districts of people, unless those people would relinquish the right of representation in the legislature: a right inestimable to them, and formidable to tyrants only.

He has called together legislative bodies at places unusual, uncomfortable, and distant from the depository of their public records, for the sole purpose of fatiguing them into compliance with his measures.

He has dissolved representative houses repeatedly for opposing, with manly firmness, his invasions on the rights of the people.

He has refused, for a long time after such dissolutions, to cause others to be elected; whereby the legislative powers, incapable of annihilation, have returned to the people at large for their exercise; the state remaining, in the meantime, exposed to all the danger of invasion from without, and convulsions within.

He has endeavored to prevent the population of these States; for that purpose, obstructing the laws for naturalization of foreigners, refusing to pass others to encourage their migration hither, and raising the conditions of new appropriations of lands.

He has obstructed the administration of justice, by refusing his assent to laws for establishing judiciary powers.

He has made judges dependent on his will alone, for the tenure of their offices, and the amount and payment of their salaries.

He has erected a multitude of new offices, and sent hither swarms of officers to harass our people, and eat out their substance.

He has kept among us, in time of peace, standing armies,

without the consent of our legislatures.

He has affected to render the military independent of, and superior to, the civil power.

He has combined, with others, to subject us to a jurisdiction foreign to our Constitution, and unacknowledged by our laws; giving his assent to their acts of pretended legislation:

For quartering large bodies of armed troops among us:

For protecting them by a mock trial, from punishment, for any murders which they should commit on the inhabitants of these States:

For cutting off our trade with all parts of the world:

For imposing taxes on us without our consent:

For depriving us, in many cases, of the benefit of trial by jury:

For transporting us beyond seas to be tried for pretended offences:

For abolishing the free system of English laws in a neighboring province, establishing therein an arbitrary government, and enlarging its boundaries, so as to render it at once an example and fit instrument for introducing the same absolute rule into these colonies:

For taking away our charters, abolishing our most valuable laws, and altering, fundamentally, the powers of our governments:

For suspending our own legislatures, and declaring themselves invested with power to legislate for us in all cases whatsoever.

He has abdicated government here, by declaring us out of his protection, and waging war against us.

He has plundered our seas, ravaged our coasts, burnt our towns, and destroyed the lives of our people.

He is, at this time, transporting large armies of foreign mercenaries to complete the works of death, desolation, and tyranny, already begun, with circumstances of cruelty and perfidy scarcely paralleled in the most barbarous ages, and totally unworthy the head of a civilized nation.

He has constrained our fellow citizens, taken captive on the high seas, to bear arms against their country, to become the executioners of their friends, and brethren, or to fall themselves by their hands.

He has excited domestic insurrections amongst us, and has endeavored to bring on the inhabitants of our frontiers, the merciless Indian savages, whose known rule of warfare is an undistinguished destruction of all ages, sexes, and conditions.

In every stage of these oppressions, we have petitioned for redress, in the most humble terms; our repeated petitions have been answered only by repeated injury. A prince, whose character is thus marked by every act which may define a tyrant, is unfit to be the ruler of a free people.

Nor have we been wanting in attention to our British brethren. We have warned them, from time to time, of attempts made by their legislature to extend an unwarrantable jurisdicion over us. We have reminded them of the circumstances of our emigration and settlement here. We have appealed to their native justice and magnanimity, and we have conjured them, by the ties of our common kindred, to disavow these usurpations, which would inevitably interrupt our connections and correspondence. They, too, have been deaf to the voice of justice and consanguinity. We must, therefore, acquiesce in the necessity which denounces our separation, and hold them, as we hold the rest of mankind, enemies in war, in peace, friends.

We, therefore, the representatives of the United States of America, in general Congress assembled, appealing to the Supreme Judge of the world for the rectitude of our intentions, do, in the name, and by the authority of the good people of these colonies, solemnly publish and declare, that these united colonies are, and of right ought to be, free and independent states: that they are absolved from all allegiance to the British Crown, and that all political connection between them and the state of Great Britain is, and ought to be, totally dissolved; and that, as free and independent states, they have full power to levy war, conclude peace, contract alliances, establish commerce, and to do all other acts and things which independent states may of right do. And, for the support of this declaration, with a firm reliance on the protection of Divine Providence, we mutually pledge to each other our lives, our fortunes, and our sacred honor.

THE CONSTITUTION
OF THE UNITED STATES

> *We the people of the United States, in order to form a more perfect union, establish justice, insure domestic tranquillity, provide for the common defense, promote the general welfare, and secure the blessings of liberty to ourselves and our posterity, do ordain and establish this Constitution for the United States of America.*

ARTICLE I

Section 1. All legislative powers herein granted shall be vested in a Congress of the United States, which shall consist of a Senate and House of Representatives.

Section 2. 1. The House of Representatives shall be composed of members chosen every second year by the people of the several States, and the electors in each State shall have the qualifications requisite for electors of the most numerous branch of the State legislature.

2. No person shall be a representative who shall not have attained to the age of twenty-five years, and been seven years a citizen of the United States, and who shall not, when elected, be an inhabitant of that State in which he shall be chosen.

3. Representatives and direct taxes[1] shall be apportioned among the several States which may be included within this Union, according to their respective numbers, which shall be determined by adding to the whole number of free persons, including those bound to service for a term of years, and excluding Indians not taxed, *three fifths of all other persons.*[2] The actual enumeration shall be made within three years after the first meeting of the Congress of the United States, and within every subsequent term of ten years, in such manner as they shall by law direct. The number of representatives shall not exceed one for every thirty thousand, but each State shall have at least one representative; and until such enumeration shall be made, the State of New Hampshire shall be entitled to choose three, Massachusetts eight, Rhode Island and Providence Plantations one, Connecticut five, New York six, New Jersey four, Pennsylvania eight, Delaware one, Maryland six, Virginia ten, North Carolina five, South Carolina five, and Georgia three.

4. When vacancies happen in the representation from any State, the executive authority thereof shall issue writs of election to fill such vacancies.

1 See the 16th Amendment.
2 See the 14th Amendment. 203

5. The House of Representatives shall choose their speaker and other officers; and shall have the sole power of impeachment.

Section 3. 1. The Senate of the United States shall be composed of two senators from each State, *chosen by the legislature thereof,*[1] for six years; and each senator shall have one vote.

2. Immediately after they shall be assembled in consequence of the first election, they shall be divided as equally as may be into three classes. The seats of the senators of the first class shall be vacated at the expiration of the second year, of the second class at the expiration of the fourth year, and of the third class at the expiration of the sixth year, so that one third may be chosen every second year; and if vacancies happen by resignation, or otherwise, during the recess of the legislature of any State, the executive thereof may make temporary appointments until the next meeting of the legislature, which shall then fill such vacancies.[1]

3. No person shall be a senator who shall not have attained to the age of thirty years, and been nine years a citizen of the United States, and who shall not, when elected, be an inhabitant of that State for which he shall be chosen.

4. The Vice President of the United States shall be President of the Senate, but shall have no vote, unless they be equally divided.

5. The Senate shall choose their other officers, and also a president *pro tempore,* in the absence of the Vice President, or when he shall exercise the office of the President of the United States.

6. The Senate shall have the sole power to try all impeachments. When sitting for that purpose, they shall be on oath or affirmation. When the President of the United States is tried, the chief justice shall preside: and no person shall be convicted without the concurrence of two thirds of the members present.

7. Judgment in cases of impeachment shall not extend further than to removal from office, and disqualifications to hold and enjoy any office of honor, trust or profit under the United States: but the party convicted shall nevertheless be liable and subject to indictment, trial, judgment and punishment, according to law.

Section 4. 1. The times, places, and manner of holding elections for senators and representatives, shall be prescribed in each State by the legislature thereof; but the Congress may at any time by law make or alter such regulations, except as to the places of choosing senators.

2. The Congress shall assemble at least once in every year, and such meeting shall be on the first Monday in December, unless they shall by law appoint a different day.

Section 5. 1. Each House shall be the judge of the elections, returns and qualifications of its own members, and a major-

---

1 See the 17th Amendment.

ity of each shall constitute a quorum to do business; but a
smaller number may adjourn from day to day, and may be
authorized to compel the attendance of absent members, in such
manner, and under such penalties as each House may provide.

2. Each House may determine the rules of its proceedings,
punish its members for disorderly behavior, and, with the concurrence of two thirds, expel a member.

3. Each House shall keep a journal of its proceedings, and
from time to time publish the same, excepting such parts as may
in their judgment require secrecy; and the yeas and nays of the
members of either House on any question shall, at the desire of
one fifth of those present, be entered on the journal.

4. Neither House, during the session of Congress, shall,
without the consent of the other, adjourn for more than three
days, nor to any other place than that in which the two Houses
shall be sitting.

Section 6. 1. The senators and representatives shall receive
a compensation for their services, to be ascertained by law, and
paid out of the Treasury of the United States. They shall in all
cases, except treason, felony, and breach of the peace, be privileged from arrest during their attendance at the session of their
respective Houses, and in going to and returning from the same;
and for any speech or debate in either House, they shall not be
questioned in any other place.

2. No senator or representative shall, during the time for
which he was elected, be appointed to any civil office under the
authority of the United States, which shall have been created,
or the emoluments whereof shall have been increased during
such time; and no person holding any office under the United
States shall be a member of either House during his continuance
in office.

Section 7. 1. All bills for raising revenue shall originate in
the House of Representatives; but the Senate may propose or
concur with amendments as on other bills.

2. Every bill which shall have passed the House of Representatives and the Senate, shall, before it becomes a law, be
presented to the President of the United States; if he approves
he shall sign it, but if not he shall return it, with his objections
to that House in which it shall have originated, who shall enter
the objections at large on their journal, and proceed to re-
consider it. If after such reconsideration two thirds of that
House shall agree to pass the bill, it shall be sent, together with
the objections, to the other House, by which it shall likewise
be reconsidered, and if approved by two thirds of that House,
it shall become a law. But in all such cases the votes of both
Houses shall be determined by yeas and nays, and the names of
the persons voting for and against the bill shall be entered on
the journal of each House respectively. If any bill shall not be
returned by the President within ten days (Sundays excepted)

after it shall have been presented to him, the same shall be a law, in like manner as if he had signed it, unless the Congress by their adjournment prevent its return, in which case it shall not be a law.

3. Every order, resolution, or vote to which the concurrence of the Senate and the House of Representatives may be necessary (except on a question of adjournment) shall be presented to the President of the United States; and before the same shall take effect, shall be approved by him, or being disapproved by him, shall be repassed by two thirds of the Senate and House of Representatives, according to the rules and limitations prescribed in the case of a bill.

Section 8. The Congress shall have the power

1. To lay and collect taxes, duties, imposts, and excises, to pay the debts and provide for the common defense and general welfare of the United States; but all duties, imposts, and excises shall be uniform throughout the United States;

2. To borrow money on the credit of the United States;

3. To regulate commerce with foreign nations, and among the several States, and with the Indian tribes;

4. To establish a uniform rule of naturalization, and uniform laws on the subject of bankruptcies throughout the United States;

5. To coin money, regulate the value thereof, and of foreign coin, and fix the standard of weights and measures;

6. To provide for the punishment of counterfeiting the securities and current coin of the United States;

7. To establish post offices and post roads;

8. To promote the progress of science and useful arts, by securing for limited times to authors and inventors the exclusive right to their respective writings and discoveries;

9. To constitute tribunals inferior to the Supreme Court;

10. To define and punish piracies and felonies committed on the high seas, and offenses against the law of nations;

11. To declare war, grant letters of marque and reprisal, and make rules concerning captures on land and water;

12. To raise and support armies, but no appropriation of money to that use shall be for a longer term than two years;

13. To provide and maintain a navy;

14. To make rules for the government and regulation of the land and naval forces;

15. To provide for calling forth the militia to execute the laws of the Union, suppress insurrections and repel invasions;

16. To provide for organizing, arming, and disciplining the militia, and for governing such part of them as may be employed in the service of the United States, reserving to the States respectively, the appointment of the officers, and the authority of

---

1 See the 16th Amendment.

training the militia according to the discipline prescribed by Congress.

17. To exercise exclusive legislation in all cases whatsoever, over such district (not exceeding ten miles square) as may, by cession of particular States, and the acceptance of Congress, become the seat of the government of the United States, and to exercise like authority over all places purchased by the consent of the legislature of the State in which the same shall be, for the erection of forts, magazines, arsenals, dockyards, and other needful buildings; and

18. To make all laws which shall be necessary and proper for carrying into execution the foregoing powers, and all other powers vested by this Constitution in the government of the United States, or in any department or officer thereof.

Section 9. 1. The migration or importation of such persons as any of the States now existing shall think proper to admit, shall not be prohibited by the Congress prior to the year one thousand eight hundred and eight, but a tax or duty may be imposed on such importation, not exceeding ten dollars for each person.

2. The privilege of the writ of *habeas corpus* shall not be suspended, unless when in cases of rebellion or invasion the public safety may require it.

3. No bill of attainder or *ex post facto* law shall be passed.

4. No capitation, or other direct, tax shall be laid, unless in proportion to the census or enumeration hereinbefore directed to be taken.[1]

5. No tax or duty shall be laid on articles exported from any State.

6. No preference shall be given by any regulation of commerce or revenue to the ports of one State over those of another: nor shall vessels bound to, or from, one State be obliged to enter, clear, or pay duties in another.

7. No money shall be drawn from the treasury, but in consequence of appropriations made by law; and a regular statement and account of the receipts and expenditures of all public money shall be published from time to time.

8. No title of nobility shall be granted by the United States: and no person holding any office of profit or trust under them, shall, without the consent of the Congress, accept of any present, emolument, office, or title, of any kind whatever, from any king, prince, or foreign State.

Section 10. 1. No State shall enter into any treaty, alliance, or confederation; grant letters of marque and reprisal; coin money; emit bills of credit; make anything but gold and silver coin a tender in payment of debts; pass any bill of attainder, *ex post facto* law, or law impairing the obligation of contracts, or grant any title of nobility.

2. No State shall, without the consent of the Congress, lay
any imposts or duties on imports or exports, except what may
be absolutely necessary for executing its inspection laws: and
the net produce of all duties and imposts laid by any State on
imports or exports, shall be for the use of the treasury of the
United States; and all such laws shall be subject to the revision
and control of the Congress.

3. No State shall, without the consent of the Congress, lay
any duty of tonnage, keep troops, or ships of war in time of
peace, enter into any agreement or compact with another State,
or with a foreign power, or engage in war, unless actually invaded, or in such imminent danger as will not admit of delay.

ARTICLE II

Section 1. 1. The executive power shall be vested in a
President of the United States of America. He shall hold his
office during the term of four years, and, together with the
Vice President, chosen for the same term, be elected as follows:

2. Each State shall appoint, in such manner as the legislature thereof may direct, a number of electors, equal to the
whole number of senators and representatives to which the State
may be entitled in the Congress: but no senator or representative, or person holding an office of trust or profit under the
United States, shall be appointed an elector.

The electors shall meet in their respective States, and vote
by ballot for two persons, of whom one at least shall not be
an inhabitant of the same State with themselves. And they
shall make a list of all the persons voted for, and of the number
of votes for each; which list they shall sign and certify, and
transmit sealed to the seat of the government of the United
States, directed to the president of the Senate. The president
of the Senate shall, in the presence of the Senate and House
of Represenatives, open all the certificates, and the votes shall
then be counted. The person having the greatest number of
votes shall be the President, if such number be a majority of the
whole number of electors appointed; and if there be more than
one who have such majority, and have an equal number of
votes, then the House of Representatives shall immediately
choose by ballot one of them for President; and if no person
have a majority, then from the five highest on the list the said
House shall in like manner choose the President. But in choosing
the President, the votes shall be taken by States, the representation from each State having one vote; a quorum for this purpose
shall consist of a member or members from two thirds of the
States, and a majority of all the States shall be necessary to a
choice. In every case, after the choice of the President, the
person having the greatest number of votes of the electors shall

be the Vice President. But if there should remain two or more who have equal votes, the Senate shall choose from them by ballot the Vice President.[1]

3. The Congress may determine the time of choosing the electors, and the day on which they shall give their votes; which day shall be the same throughout the United States.

4. No person except a natural born citizen, or a citizen of the United States, at the time of the adoption of this Constitution, shall be eligible to the office of President; neither shall any person be eligible to that office who shall not have attained to the age of thirty-five years, and been fourteen years a resident within the United States.

5. In case of the removal of the President from office, or of his death, resignation, or inability to discharge the powers and duties of the said office, the same shall devolve on the Vice President, and the Congress may by law provide for the case of removal, death, resignation, or inability, both of the President and Vice President, declaring what officer shall then act as President, and such officer shall act accordingly, until the disability be removed, or a President shall be elected.

6. The President shall, at stated times, receive for his services a compensation, which shall neither be increased nor diminished during the period for which he shall have been elected, and he shall not receive within that period any other emolument from the United States, or any of them.

7. Before he enter on the execution of his office, he shall take the following oath or affirmation:—"I do solemnly swear (or affirm) that I will faithfully execute the office of President of the United States, and will to the best of my ability, preserve, protect and defend the Constitution of the United States."

Section 2. 1. The President shall be commander in chief of the army and navy of the United States, and of the militia of the several States, when called into the actual service of the United States; he may require the opinion, in writing, of the principal officer in each of the executive departments, upon any subject relating to the duties of their respective offices, and he shall have power to grant reprieves and pardons for offenses against the United States, except in cases of impeachment.

2. He shall have power, by and with the advice and consent of the Senate, to make treaties, provided two thirds of the senators present concur; and he shall nominate, and by and with the advice and consent of the Senate, shall appoint ambassadors, other public ministers and consuls, judges of the Supreme Court, and all other officers of the United States, whose appointments are not herein otherwise provided for, and which shall be established by law: but the Congress may by law vest the appointment of such inferior officers, as they think proper, in the

1 Superseded by the 12th Amendment.

President alone, in the courts of law, or in the heads of departments.

3. The President shall have power to fill up all vacancies that may happen during the recess of the Senate, by granting commissions which shall expire at the end of their next session.

Section 3. He shall from time to time give to the Congress information of the state of the Union, and recommend to their consideration such measures as he shall judge necessary and expedient; he may, on extraordinary occasions, convene both Houses, or either of them, and in case of disagreement between them with respect to the time of adjournment, he may adjourn them to such time as he shall think proper; he shall receive ambassadors and other public ministers; he shall take care that the laws be faithfully executed, and shall commission all the officers of the United States.

Section 4. The President, Vice President, and all civil officers of the United States, shall be removed from office on impeachment for, and conviction of, treason, bribery, or other high crimes and misdemeanors.

ARTICLE III

Section 1. The judicial power of the United States shall be vested in one Supreme Court, and in such inferior courts as the Congress may from time to time ordain and establish. The judges, both of the Supreme and inferior courts, shall hold their offices during good behavior, and shall, at stated times, receive for their services, a compensation, which. shall not be diminished during their continuance in office.

Section 2. 1. The judicial power shall extend to all cases, in law and equity, arising under this Constitution, the laws of the United States, and treaties made, or which shall be made, under their authority;—to all cases affecting ambassadors, other public ministers and consuls;—to all cases of admiralty and maritime jurisdiction;—to controversies to which the United States shall be a party;—to controversies between two or more States; between a State and citizens of another State;[1]—between citizens of different States;—between citizens of the same State claiming lands under grants of different States, and between a State, or the citizens thereof, and foreign States citizens or subjects.

2. In all cases affecting ambassadors, other public ministers and consuls, and those in which a State shall be party, the Supreme Court shall have original jurisdiction. In all the other cases before mentioned, the Supreme Court shall have appellate jurisdiction, both as to law and to fact, with such exceptions, and under such regulations as the Congress shall make.

---

1 See the 11th Amendment.

3. The trial of all crimes, except in cases of impeach-ment, shall be by jury; and such trial shall be held in the State where the said crimes shall have been committed; but when not committed within any State, the trial shall be at such place or places as the Congress may by law have directed.

Section 3. 1. Treason against the United States shall consist only in levying war against them, or in adhering to their enemies, giving them aid and comfort. No person shall be convicted of treason unless on the testimony of two witnesses to the same overt act, or on confession in open court.

2. The Congress shall have power to declare the punish-ment of treason, but no attainder of treason shall work cor-ruption of blood, or forfeiture except during the life of the person attained.

ARTICLE IV

Section 1. Full faith and credit shall be given in each State to the public acts, records, and judicial proceedings of every other State. And the Congress may by general laws prescribe the manner in which such acts, records and proceed-ings shall be proved, and the effect thereof.

Section 2. 1. The citizens of each State shall be entitled to all privileges and immunities of citizens in the several States.[2]

2. A person charged in any State with treason, felony, or other crime, who shall flee from justice, and be found in another State, shall on demand of the executive authority of the State from which he fled, be delivered up to be removed to the State having jurisdiction of the crime.

3. No person held to service or labor in one State under the laws thereof, escaping into another, shall in consequence of any law or regulation therein, be discharged from such service or labor, but shall be delivered up on claim of the party to whom such service or labor may be due.[1]

Section 3. 1. New States may be admitted by the Con-gress into this Union; but no new State shall be formed or erected within the jurisdiction of any other State, nor any State be formed by the junction of two or more States, or parts of States, without the consent of the legislatures of the States concerned as well as of the Congress.

2. The Congress shall have power to dispose of and make all needful rules and regulations respecting the territory or other property belonging to the United States; and nothing in this Constitution shall be so construed as to prejudice any claims of the United States, or of any particular State.

Section 4. The United States shall guarantee to every State in this Union a republican form of government, and shall

1 See the 13th Amendment.
2 See the 14th Amendment, Sec. 1.

protect each of them against invasion; and on application of the legislature, or of the executive (when the legislature cannot be convened) against domestic violence.

ARTICLE V

The Congress, whenever two thirds of both Houses shall deem it necessary, shall propose amendments to this Constitution, or, on the application of the legislature of two thirds of the several States, shall call a convention for proposing amendments, which in either case, shall be valid to all intents and purposes, as part of this Constitution when ratified by the legislatures of three fourths of the several States, or by conventions in three fourths thereof, as the one or the other mode of ratification may be proposed by the Congress; Provided that no amendment which may be made prior to the year one thousand eight hundred and eight shall in any manner affect the first and fourth clauses in the ninth section of the first article; and that no State, without its consent, shall be deprived of its equal suffrage in the Senate.

ARTICLE VI

1. All debts contracted and engagements entered into, before the adoption of this Constitution, shall be as valid against the United States under this Constitution, as under the Confederation.[2]

2. This Constitution, and the laws of the United States which shall be made in pursuance thereof; and all treaties made, or which shall be made, under the authority of the United States, shall be the supreme law of the land; and the Judges in every State shall be bound thereby, anything in the Constitution or laws of any State to the contrary notwithstanding.

3. The senators and representatives before mentioned, and the members of the several State legislatures, and all executive and judicial officers, both of the United States and of the several States, shall be bound by oath or affirmation to support this Constitution; but no religious test shall ever be required as a qualification to any office or public trust under the United States.

ARTICLE VII

The ratification of the conventions of nine States shall be. sufficient for the establishment of this Constitution between the States so ratifying the same.

Done in Convention by the unanimous consent of the States present the seventeenth day of September in the year of our Lord one thousand seven hundred and eighty-seven, and of the independence of the United States of America the twelfth.. In witness whereof we have hereunto subscribed our names.   [Names omitted]

2 See the 14th Amendment, Sec. 4.

Articles in addition to, and amendment of, the Constitution of the United States of America, proposed by Congress, and ratified by the legislatures of the several States pursuant to the fifth article of the original Constitution.

AMENDMENTS
First Ten Amendments passed by Congress Sept. 25, 1789.
Ratified by three-fourths of the States December 15, 1791.

ARTICLE I
Congress shall make no law respecting an establishment of religion, or prohibiting the free exercise thereof; or abridging the freedom of speech, or of the press; or the right of the people peaceably to assemble, and to petition the government for a redress of grievances.

ARTICLE II
A well regulated militia, being necessary to the security of a free State, the right of the people to keep and bear arms, shall not be infringed.

ARTICLE III
No soldier shall, in time of peace be quartered in any house, without the consent of the owner, nor in time of war, but in a manner to be prescribed by law.

ARTICLE IV
The right of the people to be secure in their persons, houses, papers, and effects, against unreasonable searches and seizures, shall not be violated, and no warrants shall issue, but upon probable cause, supported by oath or affirmation, and particularly describing the place to be searched, and the persons or things to be seized.

ARTICLE V
No person shall be held to answer for a capital, or otherwise infamous crime, unless on a presentment or indictment of a grand jury, except in cases arising in the land or naval forces, or in the militia, when in actual service in time of war or public danger; nor shall any person be subject for the same offense to be twice put in jeopardy of life or limb; nor shall be compelled in any criminal case to be a witness against himself, nor be deprived of life, liberty, or property, without due process of law; nor shall private property be taken for public use without just compensation.

ARTICLE VI
In all criminal prosecutions, the accused shall enjoy the right to a speedy and public trial, by an impartial jury of the State and district wherein the crime shall have been committed, which district shall have been previously ascertained by law, and to be

informed of the nature and cause of the accusation; to be confronted with the witnesses against him; to have compulsory process for obtaining witnesses in his favor, and to have the assistance of counsel for his defense.

ARTICLE VII

In suits at common law, where the value in controversy shall exceed twenty dollars, the right of trial by jury shall be preserved, and no fact tried by a jury shall be otherwise reëxamined in any court of the United States, than according to the rules of the common law.

ARTICLE VIII

Excessive bail shall not be required, nor excessive fines imposed, nor cruel and unusual punishments inflicted.

ARTICLE IX

The enumeration in the Constitution of certain rights shall not be construed to deny or disparage others retained by the people.

ARTICLE X

The powers not delegated to the United States by the Constitution, nor prohibited by it to the States, are reserved to the States respectively, or to the people.

ARTICLE XI
Passed by Congress March 5, 1794. Ratified January 8, 1798.

The judicial power of the United States shall not be construed to extend to any suit in law or equity, commenced or prosecuted against one of the United States by citizens of another State, or by citizens or subjects of any foreign State.

ARTICLE XII
Passed by Congress December 12, 1803. Ratified September 25, 1804.

The electors shall meet in their respective States, and vote by ballot for President and Vice President, one of whom, at least, shall not be an inhabitant of the same State with themselves; they shall name in their ballots the person voted for as President, and in distinct ballots, the person voted for as Vice President, and they shall make distinct lists of all persons voted for as President and of all persons voted for as Vice President, and of the number of votes for each, which lists they shall sign and certify, and transmit sealed to the seat of the government of the United States, directed to the President of the Senate;— The President of the Senate shall, in the presence of the Senate and House of Representatives, open all the certificates and the votes shall then be counted;—The person having the greatest number of votes for President, shall be the President, if such number be a majority of the whole number of electors appointed; and if no person have such majority, then from the persons having the highest numbers not exceeding three on the list of those voted for as President, the House of Representatives shall choose immediately, by ballot, the President. But in choosing the President, the votes shall be taken by States, the representation from each State having one vote; a quorum for this purpose shall consist of a member or members from two thirds of the States, and a majority of all the States shall be necessary to a choice. And if the House of Representatives shall not choose a President whenever the right of choice shall devolve upon them, before the fourth day of March next following, then the Vice President shall act as President, as in the case of the death or other constitutional disability of the President. The person having the greatest number of votes as Vice President shall be the Vice President, if such number be a majority of the whole number of electors appointed, and if no person have a majority, then from the two highest numbers on the list, the Senate shall choose the Vice President; a quorum for the purpose shall consist of two thirds of the whole number of Senators, and a majority of the whole number shall be necessary to a choice. But no person constitutionally ineligible to the office of President shall be eligible to that of Vice President of the United States.

ARTICLE XIII
Passed by Congress February 1, 1865. Ratified December 18, 1865.

Section 1. Neither slavery nor involuntary servitude, except as punishment for crime whereof the party shall have been duly convicted, shall exist within the United States, or any place subject to their jurisdiction.

Section 2. Congress shall have power to enforce this article by appropriate legislation.

ARTICLE XIV
Passed by Congress June 16, 1866. Ratified July 23, 1868.

Section 1. All persons born or naturalized in the United States, and subject to the jurisdiction thereof, are citizens of the United States and of the State wherein they reside. No State shall make or enforce any law which shall abridge the privileges or immunities of citizens of the United States; nor shall any State deprive any person of life, liberty, or property, without due process of law; nor deny to any person within its jurisdiction the equal protection of the laws.

Section 2. Representatives shall be apportioned among the several States according to their respective numbers, counting the whole number of persons in each State, excluding Indians not taxed. But when the right to vote at any election for the choice of electors for President and Vice President of the United States, representatives in Congress, the executive and judicial officers of a State, or the members of the legislature thereof, is denied to any of the male inhabitants of such State, being twenty-one years of age, and citizens of the United States, or in any way abridged, except for participation in rebellion, or other crime, the basis of representation therein shall be reduced in the proportion which the number of such male citizens shall bear to the whole number of male citizens twenty-one years of age in such State.

Section 3. No person shall be a senator or representative in Congress, or elector of President and Vice President, or hold any office, civil or military, under the United States, or under any State, who having previously taken an oath, as a member of Congress, or as an officer of the United States, or as a member of any State legislature, or as an executive or judicial officer of any State, to support the Constitution of the United States, shall have engaged in insurrection or rebellion against the same, or given aid or comfort to the enemies thereof. But Congress may by a vote of two thirds of each House, remove such disability.

Section 4. The validity of the public debt of the United States, authorized by law, including debts incurred for payment of pensions and bounties for services in suppressing insurrection or rebellion, shall not be questioned. But neither the United States nor any State shall assume or pay any debt or obligation incurred in aid of insurrection or rebellion against the United States, or any claim for the loss or emancipation of any slave; but all such debts, obligations, and claims shall be held illegal and void.

Section 5. The Congress shall have power to enforce, by appropriate legislation, the provisions of this article.

ARTICLE XV
Passed by Congress February 27, 1869. Ratified March 30, 1870.

Section 1. The right of citizens of the United States to vote shall not be denied or abridged by the United States or by any State on account of race, color, or previous condition of servitude.

Section 2. The Congress shall have power to enforce this article by appropriate legislation.

ARTICLE XVI
Passed by Congress July 12, 1909. Ratified February 25, 1913.

The Congress shall have power to lay and collect taxes on incomes, from whatever source derived, without apportionment among the several States, and without regard to any census or enumeration.

ARTICLE XVII
Passed by Congress May 16, 1912. Ratified May 31, 1913.

The Senate of the United States shall be composed of two senators from each state, elected by the people thereof, for six years; and each senator shall have one vote. The electors in each State shall have the qualifications requisite for electors of the most numerous branch of the State legislature.

When vacancies happen in the representation of any State in the Senate, the executive authority of such State shall issue writs of election to fill such vacancies: *Provided,* That the legis' lature of any State may empower the executive thereof to make temporary appointments until the people fill the vacancies by election as the legislature may direct.

This amendment shall not be so construed as to affect the election or term of any senator chosen before it becomes,valid as part of the Constitution.

ARTICLE XVIII
Passed by Congress December 17, 1917. Ratified January 29, 1919.

After one year from the ratification of this article, the manu' facture, sale, or transportation of intoxicating liquors within, the importation thereof into, or the exportation thereof from the United States and all territory subject to the jurisdiction thereof for beverage purposes is hereby prohibited.

The Congress and the several States shall have concurrent power to enforce this article by appropriate legislation.

This article shall be inoperative unless it shall have been ratified as an amendment to the Constitution by the legislatures. of the several States, as provided in the Consitution, within seven years from the date of the submission hereof to the states by Congress.

ARTICLE XIX
Passed by Congress June 5, 1919. Ratified August 26, 1920.

The right of citizens of the United States to vote shall not be denied or abridged by the United States or by any State on account of sex.

The Congress shall have power by appropriate legislation to enforce the provisions of this article.

ARTICLE XX
Passed by Congress March 3, 1932. Ratified January 23, 1933.

Section 1. The terms of the President and Vice President shall end at noon on the 20th day of January, and the terms of Senators and Representatives at noon on the 3d day of January, of the years in which such terms would have ended if this article had not been ratified; and the terms of their successors shall then begin.

Section 2. The Congress shall assemble at least once in

every year, and such meeting shall begin at noon on the 3d day of January, unless they shall by law appoint a different day.

Section 3. If, at the time fixed for the beginning of the term of the President, the President-elect shall have died, the Vice President-elect shall become President. If a President shall not have been chosen before the time fixed for the beginning of his term, or if the President-elect shall have failed to qualify. then the Vice President-elect shall act as President until a President shall have qualified; and the Congress may by law provide for the case wherein neither a President-elect nor a Vice President-elect shall have qualified, declaring who shall then act as President, or the manner in which one who is to act shall be selected, and such person shall act accordingly until a President or Vice President shall have qualified.

Section 4. The Congress may by law provide for the case of the death of any of the persons from whom the House of Representatives may choose a President whenever the right of choice shall have devolved upon them, and for the case of the death of any of the persons from whom the Senate may choose a Vice President whenever the right of choice shall have devolved upon them.

Section 5. Sections 1 and 2 shall take effect on the 15th day of October following the ratification of this article.

Section 6. This article shall be inoperative unless it shall have been ratified as an amendment to the Constitution by the legislatures of three-fourths of the several States within seven years from the date of its submission.

ARTICLE XXI
Passed by Congress February 20, 1933. Ratified December 5, 1933.

Section 1. The Eighteenth Article of amendment to the Constitution of the United States is hereby repealed.

Section 2. The transportation or importation into any State, Territory, or possession of the United States for delivery or use therein of intoxicating liquors in violation of the laws thereof, is hereby prohibited.

Section 3. This article shall be inoperative unless it shall have been ratified as an amendment to the Constitution by conventions in the several States, as provided in the Constitution, within seven years from the date of the submission thereof to the States by the Congress.

ARTICLE XXII
Passed by Congress March 24, 1947. Ratified February 26, 1951.

Section 1. No person shall be elected to the office of the President more than twice, and no person who has held the office of President, or acted as President, for more than two years of a term to which some other person was elected President shall be elected to the office of the President more than once. But this article shall not apply to any person holding the office of President when this article was proposed by the Congress, and shall not prevent any person who may be holding the office of President, or acting as President, during the term within which this article becomes operative from holding the office of President or acting as President during the remainder of such term.

Section 2. This article shall be inoperative unless it shall have been ratified as an amendment to the Constitution by the legislatures of three-fourths of the several States within seven years from the date of its submission to the States by the Congress.

ARTICLE XXIII
Passed by Congress June 16, 1960. Ratified Mar. 29, 1961.

Section 1. The district constituting the seat of Government of the United States shall appoint in such manner as the Congress may direct:·

A number of electors of President and Vice President equal to the whole number of Senators and Representatives in Congress to which the District would be entitled if it were a State, but in no event more than the least populous State; they shall be in addition to those appointed by the States, but they shall be considered, for the purposes of election of President and Vice President, to be electors appointed by a State; and they shall meet in the District and perform such duties as provided by the twelfth article of amendment.

Section 2. The Congress shall have the power to enforce this article by appropriate legislation.

ARTICLE XXIV
Passed by Congress Aug. 27, 1962. Ratified Jan. 23, 1964

Section 1. The right of citizens of the United States to vote in any primary or other election for President or Vice President, for electors for President or Vice President, or for Senator or Representative in Congress, shall not be denied or abridged by the United States or any State by failure to pay any poll tax or other tax.

Section 2. The Congress shall have the power to enforce this article by appropriate legislation.

ARTICLE XXV
Passed by Congress Jul. 6, 1965. Ratified Feb. 10, 1967.

Section 1. In case of the removal of the President from office or of his death or resignation, the Vice President shall become President.

Section 2. Whenever there is a vacancy in the office of the Vice President, the President shall nominate a Vice President who shall take office upon confirmation by a majority vote of both Houses of Congress.

Section 3. Whenever the President transmits to the President pro tempore of the Senate and the Speaker of the House of Representatives his written declaration that he is unable to discharge the powers and duties of his office, and until he transmits to them a written declaration to the contrary, such powers and duties shall be discharged by the Vice President as Acting President.

Section 4. Whenever the Vice President and a majority of either the principal officers of the executive departments or of such other body as Congress may by law provide, transmit to the President pro tempore of the Senate and the Speaker of the House of Representatives their written declaration that the President is unable to discharge the powers and duties of his office, the Vice President shall immediately assume the powers and duties of the office as Acting President.

Thereafter, when the President transmits to the President pro tempore of the Senate and the Speaker of the House of Representatives his written declaration that no inability exists, he shall resume the powers and duties of his office unless the Vice President and a majority of either the principal officers of the executive department or of such other body as Congress may by law provide, transmit within four days to the President pro tempore of the Senate and the Speaker of the House of Representatives their written declaration that the President is unable to discharge the powers and duties of his office. Thereupon Congress shall decide the issue, assembling within forty-eight hours for that purpose if not in session. If the Congress, within twenty-one days after receipt of the latter written declaration, or, if Congress is not in session, within twenty-one days after Congress is required to assemble, determines by two-thirds vote of both Houses that the President is unable to discharge the powers and duties of his office, the Vice President shall continue to discharge the same as Acting President; otherwise, the President shall resume the powers and duties of his office.

ARTICLE XXVI
Passed by Congress March 23, 1971. Ratified June 30, 1971.

Section 1. The right of citizens of the United States, who are eighteen years of age or older, to vote shall not be denied or abridged by the United States or by any State on account of age.

Section 2. The Congress shall have power to enforce this article by appropriate legislation.

ARTICLE XXVII

Proposed Amendment passed by Congress March 22, 1972.
Congress extended the deadline for ratification by ¾ of the state
legislatures (39 months) from March 22, 1979 to June 30, 1982.

Section 1. Equality of rights under the law shall not be denied or abridged by the United States or by any state on account of sex.

Section 2. The Congress shall have the power to enforce, by appropriate legislation, the provisions of this article.

Section 3. This amendment shall take effect two years after the date of ratification.

ARTICLE XXVIII

Proposed August 22, 1978

Section 1. For purposes of representation in the Congress, election of the President and Vice President, and article V of this Constitution, the District constituting the seat of government of the United States shall be treated as though it were a State.

Section 2. The exercise of the rights and powers conferred under this article shall be by the people of the District constituting the seat of government, and as shall be provided by the Congress.

Section 3. The twenty-third article of amendment to the Constitution of the United States is hereby repealed.

Section 4. This article shall be inoperative, unless it shall have been ratified as an amendment to the Constitution by the legislatures of three-fourths of the several States within seven years from the date of its submission.

Index

223